Coping Successfully with Bipolar

Romain U. DuFour, III

ISBN 979-8-88851-998-1 (Paperback)
ISBN 979-8-88851-999-8 (Digital)

Covenant Books
11661 Hwy 707
Murrells Inlet, SC 29576
www.covenantbooks.com

Contents

Chapter 1

Listen to Your Doctor

Any individual who has bipolar disorder cannot successfully live with it without the help and assistance of a reliable psychiatrist. This is why it is imperative that the bearer of the disorder have great communication with their care provider. Most individuals who are dealing with the condition are on prescribed medication.

For many who are battling this unpredictable mental disorder, taking prescribed psychiatric medicine could become a bit of a challenge. Some psychiatric drugs could have embarrassing side effects. It is because of those unwanted side effects, such as tremors and weight gain, just to name a few conditions, that could result from taking the prescribed medication and could prove to some to be unbearable.

Personally, I understand how difficult it could become for the depressed individual to take medications that could have physical side effects that could essentially compound one's battle with bipolar disorder enormously. Individuals coping with and living with bipolar disorder must learn how to trust that one's doctor or therapist understands the mental turmoil and agony that an individual diagnosed with the psychological condition experiences on a day-to-day basis. If an individual who is coping with the disease can trust in the expertise of one's doctor or psychiatrist, then that is half the battle on the road to success over the illness.

Many people living with bipolar disorder elect not to listen to the instructions of a well-qualified doctor who specializes in the treatment of a serious psychological disorder, such as bipolar disorder. As an individual who has learned how to cope and live with bipolar disorder for approximately thirty years, I understand how imperative it is for the sufferer of the mental disorder to listen and communicate with one's doctor each time that one has a chance to visit him or her. The bearer of bipolar disorder should view one's psychiatrist or therapist as someone vital to one's recovery.

A doctor or psychiatrist who is viewed by the patient as a viable factor in one's recovery will certainly have the individual coping with bipolar disorder follow and listen to their instructions. For someone to listen to or follow the suggestions of anyone, a relationship must be built. Those who are coping with and dealing with bipolar disorder have to develop a professional and trusting relationship with the doctor who is in charge of their care.

Once an individual who is experiencing a psychological condition is assured that the doctor or therapist has their best interests at heart, trust and a relationship will soon develop. Trust is the only way that an individual who is experiencing the highs and lows of bipolar disorder will be able to recognize and listen to all of the instructions and suggestions that a doctor gives when it comes to taking the prescribed medicine. I wholeheartedly believe that trusting and listening to one's doctor is one of the key components of sustaining a level of consistency in one's mental wholeness.

Some who have been living with and coping with bipolar disorder for a substantial time might feel as though they are experts on the condition. I believe that over time, the depressed individual can develop more knowledge about their mental disorder, but I personally do not think that when knowledge is obtained, the depressed individual is all of a sudden an expert on the condition. Psychiatrists, as well as other mental health professionals, have received extensive training on psychological illnesses such as bipolar disorder.

A patient does not typically know more about an illness than a doctor who has put in the time in perfecting their knowledge of a particular illness or disorder. Since I have been in the midst of coping with the disorder, I have gained a newfound respect for the suggestions and opinions of my doctor. No patient who is experiencing the signs and symptoms of bipolar disorder can initially tell the doctor about the efficacy of a new psychological drug that has been approved for use.

Many people living with bipolar disorder are creative and intelligent individuals. With the knowledge and information-crazed Internet, there are many bearers of the condition who are playing amateur psychiatrists. It is due to the information on the Internet that some sufferers elect to listen to their own diagnosis and prognosis instead of an experienced doctor or therapist.

One does not realize how one is living precariously when one naively thinks that one knows all there is to know about one's illness. Those who are know-it-alls regarding their psychological condition are setting themselves up for failure. The reason I am stating this is that some who ignorantly think that they know everything about their condition will, in many cases, disregard the expertise of a licensed and well-trained mental health expert.

Bipolar disorder is a mental health condition that is best coped with when depressed individuals will allow themselves to listen to the expert opinion of their doctor or therapist. One cannot maintain consistency in one's mental health by only listening to one's own limited knowledge of the disorder. Initially, when an individual who is experiencing the symptoms of the disease reaches out for help at the beginning of their bout with the disease, that individual will desperately listen to the instructions of the doctor to help them cope with the mental discomfort.

After the depressed individual becomes somewhat mentally stable, in some cases, that individual will no longer feel the need to listen and take heed to the doctor's suggestions. If your doctor says that you should abstain from alcohol and other chemical substances when taking the prescribed psychiatric medication, then I suggest that you listen. There is a reason an individual who is taking medication for bipolar disorder should not combine the medicine with other substances, which could worsen the condition. A depressed individual must listen to all of the sage advice of their doctor or therapist because that individual is unqualified to know all that the mental disorder encompasses, though knowledge is readily available.

In my opinion, I believe that listening to one's psychiatrist or therapist is extremely beneficial. One of the benefits of a depressed individual taking heed to the advice and suggestions of one's doctor is limited visits to the psychiatric hospital. When an individual who is diagnosed with bipolar disorder listens to their doctor, it can essentially save the bearer a great deal of heartache.

As an individual who also suffers from bipolar disorder, I have experienced all of the various peaks and valleys with regard to this illness. There were times when I did not want to listen to what my doctor was saying. It was because of my own stubbornness at times that a visit to the hospital became the end result.

This mental disorder requires the individual who is suffering from it to pay close attention to everything that might help the bearer of the disease overcome it and live as normal a life as possible. During the years in which I have been living with and coping with the condition, I have learned that, in many instances, the doctor knows best. I can recall some years ago when one of my former psychiatrists suggested that I journal.

After this particular doctor made that suggestion, initially I did not see the point in doing it. My skepticism decreased when I realized how writing my personal thoughts on paper really became a form of therapy. Also, writing grew into a passion once familiarity with doing it for a significant time commenced.

It was through journaling and writing that I finally found my calling. Sometimes, I think about where I would be if I did not listen to the mental health professional who initially suggested that I write my thoughts and feelings down. Journaling can help an individual who is coping with bipolar disorder gain insight into where they were mentally at a specific time in their life.

Hopefully, when the depressed individual is jotting down their innermost thoughts, it will help them cope and understand their triggers and emotions. One will have a greater chance of successfully progressing in their battle over the disorder when one can share their own unbiased personal feelings with themselves. An individual who is living with bipolar disorder should incorporate some form of journaling into their daily schedule and routine.

For some who are coping with and dealing with this challenging mental condition, emotions can become difficult to express. If the depressed individual's psychiatrist or therapist suggests that one should journal, do not disregard or dismiss it. One's life could drastically change for the better when a suggestion, such as journaling, from a doctor or therapist, is welcomed.

Depressed individuals must remain committed to the suggestion of journaling by their psychiatrist to express how they're feeling during the therapy sessions. I believe wholeheartedly that when an individual who is dealing with and living with bipolar disorder can convey to the doctor how they are feeling mentally, growth and recovery can thrive. Improvement never occurs without listening to the wise suggestions of the experts, which could dramatically affect the life of the depressed individual.

Most psychiatrists and therapists understand the signs, triggers, and symptoms of bipolar disorder. As a patient, the individual might not become aware of their own behavior. This is why it is imperative that the patient, doctor, or therapist have a genuine and trusting working relationship.

A doctor or therapist will typically have no judgment or bias when dealing with individuals who are battling with bipolar disorder. I believe that most mental health professionals get into psychiatry to help individuals who might be suffering from the condition improve and have functioning lives. When an individual is initially diagnosed with a psychiatric condition, they do not have the tools to deal with it.

The job of the psychiatrist or therapist is to help guide the individual coping with the disease to gain some semblance of independence. Bipolar disorder, in some extremely negative cases, can make the bearer of the illness remain unmotivated and stagnate. If the individual who is living and experiencing the condition develops a listening ear for how the psychiatrist or therapist can help them assemble into the world and society, I guarantee that the depressed individual will learn how to cope successfully with the condition as well as the pressures of daily living.

Individuals who have experienced the most success in coping with and dealing with this unpredictable mental disorder have allowed themselves to listen to all of the instructions and suggestions of their mental healthcare specialist. I am aware that in some instances a depressed individual might not initially agree with the suggestions and instructions of their doctor or therapist, but when improvement commences after listening to them, I am certain that the individual coping with the illness will be glad that they ultimately "buckled down and listened." It is not always easy to listen to anyone, especially with regard to one's lifestyle.

Before I was personally able to improve mentally, I had to make several lifestyle changes that I now credit my current doctor for. He suggested two simple changes in my life that I needed to make to remain consistent with my mental health. The first suggestion that he posed was that I get an adequate amount of sleep.

Another suggestion that he brought to my attention was losing weight and exercising. I must admit that when I initially heard those suggestions from him, I was oblivious to how vital these simple daily and nightly routines would eventually be helping me maintain and sustain consistency in my mood and overall health. As sufferers of bipolar disorder, there are times when we may not realize that a suggestion from a doctor or therapist is for our own benefit and good. Some patients choose not to listen to what their mental health specialist suggests because they do not want to admit that their doctor's suggestions are actually true. Those who refuse to listen and take heed to what their mental health provider suggests can ultimately be setting themselves up for experiencing negative consequences.

Knowledge about bipolar disorder is only obtained when the depressed individual is able to listen to their doctor. When the individual coping with the disorder listens, he or she can become more knowledgeable about the various terminologies and symptoms of the illness. It is imperative that the bearer of bipolar disorder gain as much knowledge as they can about their condition.

The individual who can listen to what their doctor says about all of the signs and triggers of their mental disorder will not only acquire knowledge but also become better equipped to endure the mental health battle. One who takes heed to the doctor can potentially cope with the disease without experiencing a plethora of negative setbacks. Anyone who is facing the battle of their mind must never cease listening to all of the things that their doctor suggests.

Listening to the advice of the doctor allows the depressed individual to have continuous success in coping and dealing with the life-long struggle to remain mentally stable. I believe that I have remained consistently stable in my mind for several years because I decided to take heed of my doctor's voice of reason. Sometimes, in coping with the psychiatric condition, it can become tempting to listen to one's own voice when one becomes better psychologically.

We all must learn each day that we are fortunate enough to live. To learn effectively, one must be able to listen. If one cannot listen to one's doctor, then one might as well remain in the same mental state that one initially had when one realized that one needed professional help.

It is a sign of disrespect when a depressed individual does not listen to all of the instructions and suggestions from their doctor. Every psychiatrist or therapist who treats an individual coping with bipolar disorder should be given the respect that they deserve. Individuals who refuse to listen are essentially acting as though they received the same education and training as their mental health specialist.

Not listening to the sage advice of a board certified psychiatrist or therapist can figuratively have the individual suffering from the illness "fall over the cliff." Also, no individual who is living with bipolar disorder can afford to drift deeper into a precarious psychological state. Becoming more mentally unstable is usually the result of the individual who is experiencing the negative aspect of the condition taking their illness into their own hands.

A depressed individual must listen to the doctor when he or she says that you must take medication for a substantial amount of time. So many depressed individuals disregard their own mental health and wellness when they decide that they can wean themselves off of psychotropic medicine alone. Depressed individuals who decide to do that are essentially being selfish and irresponsible. Personally, I have been guilty in the past of weaning myself off of a medication without listening to the wise opinion of the doctor, and it was because of my error in judgment that I could have potentially negatively affected my mental progress.

Yes, it is true that a doctor or therapist cannot physically force an individual who is coping with bipolar disorder to take the prescribed medicine. Some who are experiencing the illness have the mindset that no one can tell them anything. I believe this negative attitude and mindset will eventually hinder the individual who is coping with the uncertainty of the disorder.

Bipolar disorder will damage the life of the individual who is living with it if he or she refuses to listen. As a result of the damage that this mental disease could potentially cause, the result could prove deadly. In the past, I was one of the depressed individuals who did not believe in coping with the condition with medication.

I cannot personally speak for the millions of people in this country and worldwide who are coping with and dealing with this psychologically challenging disorder. What I do know is that, at times, the signs and triggers of this severe mental illness can suddenly come upon an individual. Individuals who are battling this psychiatric condition cannot successfully cope with it without treatment and counseling.

I can recall years ago when I asked the psychiatrist that I was seeing at the time the secret to staying well. He honestly revealed to me that the key to remaining mentally stable is counseling and medication management. The conversation I had with him has remained in my mind for many years.

In hindsight, I am thankful and glad that I eventually listened to what my former mental health specialist stated would be one of the key factors in coping and living successfully with this mental condition. When I finally bought into the idea of coping with this psychological illness in the long term, my condition improved tremendously. If I had refused to listen to how I could remain consistently mentally whole, I probably would not have been able to enjoy many years of mental stability and wellness.

Most psychiatrists and therapists with years of experience treating psychological conditions, such as bipolar disorder, are worth listening to. They have put in hours of sacrifice to treat individuals with mental health difficulties. I believe that it is because of many of the doctors' and mental health professionals' dedication and sacrifice over the years that a patient can at least listen to them and give these mental health experts a chance.

Some individuals are experiencing the bipolar battle who are viewing their doctor or mental health specialist as a common enemy. Those who view one's mental health care provider in that negative light will do everything else but listen to what one's care provider might advise. Viewing one's doctor or psychiatrist in that way is never positive or beneficial to a depressed individual's overall mental improvement.

It is human nature to listen to and gravitate toward individuals we like and trust. With regard to fondness and trust, many will tend to value the opinion of those whom we might consider to have good intentions toward us. One cannot listen and successfully cope with bipolar disorder when the mental health care provider is viewed as an antagonist.

Mental health professionals and specialists are there for any individuals who might be struggling with mental health. These particular individuals are truly helpful guides in the bipolar battle. In fact, they are to be trusted, listened to, and commended for helping many who are battling the disorder to remain mentally well.

I believe that many who are struggling with bipolar disorder are unaware of how vital coping, as well as listening, could become to their mental health. Without being able to listen to a reliable psychiatrist or therapist, there is no way that a depressed individual can mentally become successful. Once an individual who is coping and experiencing bipolar disorder fully decides that they will seek and listen to all that the mental health specialist suggests, then there is potentially a clear path to taking a turn for the better regarding the depressed individual experiencing a life of joy.

There are a plethora of mental health providers who truly care for their clients or patients. Although a doctor-patient relationship should be strictly professional and not personal, the patient who listens to the doctor's *do*s and *don't*s is expressing to their psychiatrist or doctor that they care when they listen and rely heavily upon all of the sound expertise of the mental healthcare provider. Do not mistake me; doctors are also humans who can sometimes be wrong from time to time.

Just because they (doctors and therapists) have the potential to make mistakes at times, that does not mean that they should not be listened to. Like any individual who is deemed to be an expert, there is always the potential for mental health professionals to either misdiagnose or overlook the signs and symptoms of an individual who is suffering from a severe mental illness.

When it comes to a psychiatrist diagnosing an individual with bipolar disorder, the signs and symptoms are usually universal. In most cases, the majority of individuals who have a diagnosis of bipolar disorder will be carefully observed. If an individual is seeking some type of mental health assistance, that individual knows mentally that something within them is not right.

The psychiatrist or mental health expert who has the task of revealing the client's or patient's diagnosis will have that individual's full attention and listening ear. An individual who is eager to put a name to the health condition in which they are experiencing does not have any other choice but to listen to the final diagnosis that the doctor has determined. After the mental health expert has determined that one is displaying some of the signs and symptoms of bipolar disorder, the depressed individual must immediately listen to the expert with hope and optimism that the disease can be treated and controlled.

Every individual who has ever been diagnosed with bipolar disorder had various experiences with the condition. Today, most cases regarding the illness are mainly treatable. What the depressed individual must become aware of is the fact that the best way to receive optimum treatment is by listening and asking relevant questions about how to cope with and overcome the mental disease.

No one can learn about one's triggers and symptoms without the aid and assistance of a mental health professional. One who can recognize and observe their own conduct and behavior can only do that when communication is expressed. Communication is best expressed when both parties are participating in the listening process.

I believe that communication between a doctor and a patient or client works best when listening is reciprocal. What I mean by reciprocal is that both the doctor and patient take turns listening. As I have matured in age, I have realized how listening can become an art form.

Have you ever tried to talk and listen at the same time? For many, it is almost impossible to listen to what someone is saying while also trying to get their point across. The signals that are relayed through our ears cannot make out the words that another individual is also saying when two people are talking simultaneously. In other words, the lines of communication are lost.

When a depressed individual is in the mental health expert's office and the expert is either writing down what they are saying or reciting verbatim what the depressed individual is telling them, that mental health professional is really listening to every word the patient/client is uttering. This is a beautiful thing for the depressed individual when he or she is heard. We all would like to be heard by someone fair and unbiased in their judgment.

This is one of the main reasons counseling and therapy have astronomically risen in the last several years, even among those who do not have a mental challenge or disorder. I believe that the best therapy sessions are when the patient/client does not dominate the session by talking nonstop throughout it. In extreme cases of mania in a bipolar individual, getting the depressed individual to communicate by listening can become a bit of a chore for the psychiatrist or therapist.

I can recall some time ago when one of my family members expressed to me that I needed to work on my listening. When this particular family member told me that, I was initially offended and upset. One day, it clicked and dawned on me that I needed to do more listening and less talking.

Since it was brought to my attention many years ago that I needed to work on my listening skills, I am now eager to do it. As I previously stated, one cannot learn anything in life while talking "a mile a minute." With listening and talking, there is so much to give and take.

Though one gives the information by conveying the message to the listener, the other person takes that information into their mind and brain. Listening to the individual who is coping with and living with bipolar disorder can also become viewed as "brain food." So the next time that you are dealing with a manic phase of the disorder, try to feed your mind by slowing your thoughts and making an effort to listen more attentively in your therapy sessions.

Typically, an individual who is coping with and living with bipolar disorder is in good hands with a reliable mental health expert. Depressed individuals must strive to feel comfortable with their psychiatrist or therapist. Once one who is suffering from a psychological disorder gains familiarity with the mental health professional, there is a potential for that individual to trust and listen to the doctor.

I cannot stress enough how crucial it is for a depressed individual to do all that is required by a licensed mental health expert to remain healthy. Taking prescribed psychotropic medicine is not as bad as one might think when the medicine is the right fit for the individual battling the disorder. The main issue between most doctors and their patients with regard to the treatment of this psychological condition is medication management.

For individuals who are dealing with the signs and symptoms of this psychological disorder, I suggest not having a stubborn and prideful mindset and attitude. Those who have that attitude will not listen to their doctor, even when the expert's suggestions are the right thing to do. As a fellow sufferer of bipolar disorder, I also had to disregard my stubborn pride and listen.

Personally, I think that many who are coping with and suffering from this unpredictable psychological condition are, in many cases, set in their ways. It is not the job of the psychiatrist or therapist to guide the depressed individual each day by putting pressure and ultimatums on them to take prescribed medicine that can potentially positively affect their lives.

Life is difficult to navigate through when an individual does not have a psychological condition. Individuals journeying through life with mental illness must take full advantage of all the help available to them. Some bearers of bipolar disorder might have to "hit rock bottom" before they change their stance by taking heed to the opinions and suggestions of a well-qualified mental health professional.

I am cognizant of the fact that the process of entrusting one's mental health treatment to a doctor or therapist can initially become nerve-racking and scary. Many of us have a fear of the unknown. If the depressed individual can go into therapy and treatment with the goal of becoming better not only for a moment but also for life, I believe that a positive breakthrough in coping with the mental health disorder will occur.

Before an individual can cope successfully and consistently with bipolar disorder, they must do their part. What I mean by the individual doing his or her part is that they must do all that they can by following the instructions and goals that they and their psychiatrist or doctor have discussed or agreed upon. After one has listened to and followed the advice and suggestions of their mental health specialist, the bearer of the illness can develop and maintain a clear conscience, knowing that they took notice and listened to what the mental health provider has suggested in their mental health plan.

Following the plans and advice of anyone can be difficult. It is in our human nature to conclude that our way of doing things is what is best for us. Bipolar disorder, like many other illnesses and conditions in this world and society, requires a keen listening ear to combat, overcome, and live successfully with it.

Many make the unwise decision to cope with and deal with this severe mental illness by becoming their own mental therapist. A sufferer of bipolar disorder is extremely unqualified and mentally unfit to cope with the illness by their own ways and standards. Those who listen only to themselves are essentially setting themselves up for doom and failure.

As an individual who might be struggling with trying to remain well, you might not see the need to listen to your doctor, but others around you can see the need. Some are sadly coping with their mental health struggles and issues by themselves.

Good-quality mental health care from a doctor or therapist is threatened by the effects of the aftermath of the viral pestilence. With many businesses having to close, including some psychiatric offices, adequate mental health care is now becoming a challenge to remain in business. Psychiatrists and mental health experts are in high demand because of the mental toll that this world and society have experienced in recent years. No one who is battling bipolar disorder can cope with it successfully without listening to what their psychiatrist suggests, especially in the state of the world that we live in today.

This is definitely the time to hone one's craft of listening. If you are fortunate enough to still see a doctor or certified mental health professional, then count your blessings. Many in our society do not receive quality mental health care because of a lack of insurance, which stems from being unemployed, as a result of the nationwide recession in which this country is unfortunately in.

Individuals who were diagnosed with bipolar disorder prepandemic should now be more receptive to following the doctor's advice. Now more than ever, a depressed individual's life does depend on how well the individual listens to how to use coping mechanisms that a doctor or therapist teaches them. Not only are therapy and medication management important to the continual success of an individual living with and being treated for bipolar disorder, but the depressed person must also rely on their listening ears by filling them up with positive and uplifting things.

Hopefully, the individual who is facing the lifelong battle of bipolar disorder has a well-meaning and supportive doctor/therapist to listen to. In the current world, a phone call or virtual visit to their mental health therapist is just as good as seeing them face-to-face or in person. Regardless of how the communication or interaction is expressed, an individual who is coping with bipolar disorder can still live successfully with it by listening to their doctor, despite the world's negativity.

Chapter 2

Be Honest with What Triggers You

Recognizing the people, places, or things that trigger you is vital to coping with bipolar disorder. Once triggers are identified, it is up to the depressed individual to either avoid or deal with them. Try to talk to someone you trust to cope with them. Individuals who are living with a severe mental illness such as bipolar disorder must be honest with themselves about what triggers them to have the potential of experiencing either a manic or depressive episode.

Many years ago, I was the type of individual who would frequent nightclubs. The atmosphere surrounding most nightclubs is one of dim lights and alcohol. Although I have not been in an actual nightclub or bar for approximately twenty years, I now know that it is a place that serves no purpose for me. When I reflect on times in my life when I would indulge in drinking alcoholic beverages, I was always at a party or nightclub where alcohol was readily available.

Before I became stricken with bipolar disorder, alcohol was always around. Whether I was at a picnic or gathering, there was always someone offering it to me. Now I know what you may be thinking; you may be thinking to yourself that during that time I could have refused the beverage and said "no." Because of peer pressure and the fact that I was so young and easily influenced, I probably did not have the motivation and willpower to refuse.

Today, as an individual with sobriety and success in coping with and living with bipolar disorder, I will not allow myself to indulge in any kind of alcoholic drinking whatsoever. This is not to say that if someone offers me alcohol now, I will immediately become weak and disregard the hard work it took for me to get to the point of not succumbing to the trigger of being around those who consume alcohol. For any individual who is coping with any type of severe mental illness, it is usually during the initial therapy session that a psychiatrist or therapist should bring to the depressed person's attention that it is not at all wise or beneficial to drink any kind of alcoholic beverage, which also includes wine.

Some people who are diagnosed with bipolar disorder might not have alcohol as one of their triggers. With regard to a potential trigger, it can come in the form of a certain toxic individual who might have been prominent in their life at a certain point in time. My hope for the individual with that particular trigger is that the individual affected recognizes the other individual as a trigger and potential threat to their mental wellness and wholeness. For example, if an individual is constantly argumentative toward you, then that individual is a live trigger.

Replacing that trigger person with someone who is caring, supportive, and less argumentative is the key to becoming less triggered and mentally well. Identifying one's triggers should not become burdensome for the individual living with bipolar disorder. If it means having peace of mind and enjoying many days of consistency in one's mental health, then one's triggers must be addressed.

Support systems and journaling are imperative when it comes to dealing with and identifying triggers. There is nothing like a trusted confidant to whom one can express their triggers to make a depressed individual feel more comfortable. Sometimes an individual may not be cognizant of the person, place, or thing that could pose a threat to their mental stability.

Triggers in life are just that. They are toxic threats that can damage or harm one's mental progress. When dealing with a mental illness, such as bipolar disorder, an individual must not feel harmed or threatened in any way.

If the depressed person has those feelings, he or she should feel comfortable telling someone whom they trust how they are feeling, or if there is not someone like that around, they should not hesitate to put it on paper. No individual is wrong about the people, places, and things in this world that could essentially become a mental threat. Today, I can only imagine all of the triggers that could potentially negatively affect an individual coping with this psychiatric condition.

When it comes to things that could trigger an individual, I am not certain that these triggers will ever fully go away. Traumatic experiences in life can be triggered by anything. A person, a movie, or a television program can send one back to the negative mental state that they experienced a plethora of years ago.

In other words, there is some semblance of nostalgia when it comes to having triggers. Mental recognition is the key to identifying them. We all know what makes us either happy or sad.

Anxiety can result from an individual becoming triggered by a situation or circumstance. Any kind of anxiety from a trigger can have a devastating impact on the individual who suffers from any psychological condition, let alone bipolar disorder. This is why it is extremely beneficial to the depressed individual when he or she can identify many of the things in life that trigger them.

Doctors and patients working together can identify the people, places, and things that contribute to the psychological threats to one's mental wholeness and wellness. It is through intense counseling and therapy that an individual can be informed about how to behave and react when triggers surface. The question is not whether the trigger will occur; the question is when.

Therapy can teach any individual how to remain calm when triggered. For instance, there are breathing techniques that one could learn from their doctor or therapist after being triggered, which may have resulted in some type of anxiety or mental agony. In the midst of becoming triggered, the depressed individual should strive not to panic or succumb to it.

Being honest with oneself is both crucial and beneficial in combating and coping with triggers that can affect one's mental well-being. One's reaction is important regarding how triggers in life are dealt with. Never allow your triggers to derail your chances of trying to remain psychologically healthy and fit.

Overcoming triggers in life is essential to coping with bipolar disorder. Bipolar disorder is an illness that can be triggered without a moment's notice. Once the depressed individual gains mastery over what triggers them, then success over the mental disorder will gradually occur.

The process of overcoming one's triggers does not occur suddenly. Intensive therapy and honesty with oneself are needed if the individual who is coping with bipolar disorder wants to gain control over the psychological threats to their mental wellness. If one's trigger is identified and coped with, then another trigger can also be overcome.

I recall this one specific time when I was in the psychiatric hospital and I became someone's trigger. There was an older gentleman who innocently asked me where I was originally from. When I revealed to him that I was a native of the city of New Orleans, he immediately had a different tone and demeanor.

Because he had a negative experience when he visited that city, I soon became his nemesis. No matter how kind and positive I was toward him, he could not overcome the negative experience that happened to him in that particular town. In fact, he blamed me the whole time that I was in his presence for being from the very town where he experienced those negative occurrences.

Every social interaction that I had with him became so difficult to bear that I personally feared for my life during that time. This man's anger and hostility could not be tamed simply because I said I was from a specific town that brought up negative memories for him.

Since I triggered a painful and negative experience in him because of where I was from, this older man also wanted to inflict all of his pain on me. His trigger ultimately turned into a blind obsession. In this gentleman's mind, I represented pain, struggle, and discomfort all at once.

Now it remains to be seen if this particular gentleman ever overcame his personal trigger of anyone being from the city where he experienced so much chaos and turmoil. Though I was dealing with my own issues and problems, I must state that I felt empathy and sympathy for this triggered man. Hopefully, if this particular gentleman is still alive, my hope for him is that he finally comes to terms with his negative experience.

Mental health specialists are there to help anyone overcome those past triggers. Of course, I am not a doctor or therapist, but I have had approximately thirty years of personal experience dealing with and coping with the various triggers and symptoms of this psychological illness. During the time that I have been living with bipolar disorder, I have gained more knowledge and insight into the people, places, and things that could threaten my mental health. Triggers in life can become detrimental to the depressed individual's mental growth, but when the individual can remember how they overcame their past trigger(s), then they have the potential to acquire hope.

Manic and depressive episodes are part of the individual who is experiencing the disorder. In my experience with being manic, I am now aware that worry and a lack of sleep trigger this particular episode. I personally recall how I felt when the manic phase of the illness manifested itself.

During my experience of being overwhelmed with deep sadness and despair, I remember how being disappointed by people who I deeply loved triggered this extreme mood of darkness and hopelessness. These feelings and emotions I just described can only be triggered when the depressed individual is the most vulnerable. One has to strive to be honest with the individual from within to combat the people and things in life that can potentially become negative triggers.

I believe that depressed individuals can overcome life's triggers when they learn from the trigger that results in an unfavorable experience. In the past, it was difficult to identify the triggers that could send me into a negative mental state because, during that time in my life, I did not want to relive those situations and circumstances that ended in pain. So instead of focusing on those unwanted triggers, I decided to mentally avoid them by blocking them out.

Suppressing triggers can become harmful to the depressed individual in the long run. Sometimes, an individual can unknowingly suppress painful triggers, which results in anger and resentment. Individuals who are coping with bipolar disorder must somehow find the courage and strength to face the painful triggers of life.

Progress and consistency in this psychological condition cannot be established until the depressed individual deals with all of the negative triggers that influence them to be either in a manic or depressive state. This will require work on the depressed individual's part. I believe that therapy, internal insight, and examination are the only ways that an individual can move on from allowing the triggers in their life to have precedence and dominion over them.

Previously, I discussed how imperative it is for an individual who is suffering from bipolar disorder to develop trust in their doctor or mental health specialist. Psychiatrists who specialize in healing the whole person will emphasize how vital it is for the depressed individual to commence with the bothersome triggers that pose a long-term threat to their psychological state. Triggers that are emphasized during the counseling sessions are beneficial when they come to fruition in the depressed individual's daily interactions.

I personally credit my consistency of success in coping with this unpredictable psychological disorder with my willingness to allow myself to recollect those people, places, and things that trigger me into having a manic or depressive episode. Now I am not stating that one continues to harbor those negative experiences of the past, but what I am saying to the individual who is trying to turn the corner in coping with their illness is to always remember what triggers them in the back of their mind. If one continues to enjoy life despite their triggers having the potential to cause havoc mentally, then their triggers can become less of a concern.

Life itself is a series of emotional triggers. Unfortunately, they are inevitable. Triggers such as people and situations do not cease just because an individual is diagnosed with bipolar disorder.

Coping with triggers effectively requires commitment and mental growth. One has to be committed to recognizing the things in life that might serve as negative triggers. Without becoming fully on board with the identification of triggers in one's life, the depressed individual can potentially remain in the same negative mental position.

A trigger left unattended can manifest into a full-blown problem. For example, some who disregard the things in life that can become triggers are living in denial. An individual who lives that way is not transparent and honest with themselves.

To successfully cope and overcome bipolar disorder, depressed individuals must be as honest as possible with their feelings and emotions. When it comes to living with any type of illness or sickness, honesty with oneself will always give the individual experiencing it a chance to successfully live with the condition. This is why it is imperative for the individual living with bipolar disorder to accept the fact that triggers play a significant role in the mental disease.

No individual who is coping with bipolar disorder should become convinced that their triggers need to be addressed truthfully and carefully. It is difficult to identify triggers without the aid of a viable mental health professional. Though it is not impossible for a depressed individual to recognize the potential of another individual or situation to trouble them, an individual can still learn what could potentially become a trigger for them on their own.

When I was in the midst of my manic phase some time ago, I initially did not realize that a lack of adequate rest would be a leading contributor to my own bouts of mania. It took some time for me to understand how sleep deprivation is the dominant trigger for feeling anxious and manic. Now that I realize how important it is to not become triggered by trying to stay up all night, I am determined to sleep no less than six hours overnight.

After it dawned on me that sleepless nights are a trigger for experiencing a manic episode, I commenced taking proper care of myself by making sleep a mandatory priority in my life. It also helps that my psychiatrist will usually ask me at the genesis of our therapy session about my nightly sleep pattern. Any individual who is diagnosed with bipolar disorder can become negatively affected by the condition when they choose to put the need for a sufficient amount of rest on the backburner.

If being triggered by a lack of proper rest was not important in one's life as a bearer of bipolar disorder, then most psychiatrists and mental health professionals would not have included the question of one's sleep patterns on the form that is filled out, generally, before the depressed individual goes into a therapy or counseling session. The trigger for many who are stricken by this psychological condition is a lack of sleep. Typically, this is a common and universal trigger for the individual who is affected by the manic phase of the illness.

You have to personally decide if you will continue to journey through life being triggered by the slightest situation or circumstance. A life easily triggered is not a content and happy one. Triggers in life can disturb an individual's peace of mind.

With regard to triggers, sometimes they can evolve or diminish over time. Some triggers affected me in a certain way when I was younger, but now those particular triggers do not have the same effect on me as they once did. Sadly, some will navigate through life without ever being able to release triggers that become difficult and burdensome.

If one is not careful, triggers can become so cancerous in one's life that they will affect the individual for a lifetime. My hope for anyone who is experiencing the burden of triggers is to not lose faith while in the midst of experiencing them. In life, many situations and circumstances can put a damper on one's emotions.

Unfortunately, no one has the power to predict when one will be triggered by something. Because of the unpredictability and uncertainty of triggers, it can influence an individual to "live on the edge." Personally, I cannot decide when and where a potential trigger can pop up.

An individual who desires to live and cope successfully with bipolar disorder must remain vigilant. That individual should monitor their own emotional triggers quite frequently. Monitoring emotional triggers effectively will result in the individual finally being able to get them under control.

What can make vigilance difficult with regard to emotions and triggers is the depressed individual's internal thoughts and mindset. Although we are advanced as a society, no one can read the mind of any individual. Because psychiatrists and mental health experts are not "mind readers," they can only evaluate the depressed individual by the individual's conduct and behavior.

Sometimes the emotionally triggered individual will exhibit a great deal of irritability. Those who are irritated are typically the most miserable. I am certain that no one desires to live their life in that fashion.

Bipolar disorder is a psychological condition that will leave the individual struggling with and coping with the disorder irritated, frustrated, and miserable when triggers are not properly assessed and honestly identified. My suggestion to the individual who is battling emotional triggers in their head is to deal with them directly. No issue or problem in life is ever overcome when it is "swept under the rug."

Think about the great satisfaction one will experience when one's battle with emotional triggers is eventually overcome. Overcoming triggers in one's life does not mean that they (triggers) are gone forever. Though the triggers can remain dormant for a significant time in the mind of the bearer of bipolar disorder, time can also serve as a great ally when the emotional trigger loses its mental and emotional grasp

Coping with triggers is crucial to remaining well with regard to this sometimes-uncontrollable mental disorder. The goal for any individual living with bipolar disorder is to not allow their triggers to get the best of them. Although this mental condition is different from post-traumatic stress, which is predicated on experiencing triggers that could result in horrific anxiety and episodes, when the depressed individual living with bipolar disorder does not have their triggers under control, it can also have a profound effect on their minds.

If one is experiencing emotional triggers while being diagnosed with bipolar disorder, do not hesitate to talk about them. For those who are negatively affected by triggers, some may feel embarrassed or ashamed to discuss the things that could become emotional threats to their mental health out of fear of being judged. To remain mentally well, the depressed individual must move past those feelings of shame.

We all go through some type of trauma at some point in our lives. Bipolar disorder can be difficult to treat when the individual suffering from it refuses to discuss with the psychiatrist or mental health expert those emotional triggers that make the client go from being relatively calm to being amplified and aggravated. Our emotions are extremely important to our mental wellness.

Though bipolar disorder is a psychological and mental health condition, it is also heavily based on one's emotional state. Emotions that are out of order will lead an individual to potentially have a psychotic or mental breakdown. Experiencing a mental breakdown is scary and difficult, especially for the friends and loved ones of the individual who is affected by it.

Triggers that are not dealt with in a therapeutic setting can result in an individual having an emotional breakdown. This is why depressed individuals must allow themselves to express to the doctor or therapist everything that can become a potential risk for their feelings and emotions. Whether one is an emotional person or not, every individual's emotions should be valid.

An individual who is affected by bipolar disorder can be highly triggered by anything. It is because of this potential threat to one's emotions that the bearer of the disorder learns how to recognize when they are triggered. Triggers will continue to negatively affect one's emotional state if the depressed individual cannot identify where they are coming from.

The depressed individual must delve deep from within to overcome those bothersome emotional triggers. Overcoming triggers in one's life requires patience, understanding, and courage. Some may find it too difficult and unappealing to identify the source of their psychological threats.

Nothing in life is easy. Identifying, recognizing, and resolving emotional triggers in therapy may require a plethora of years. As an individual who has experienced psychological counseling for a significant period, when the origin of those triggers is finally identified, it is truly well worth the time and effort.

Years ago, I was not personally ready to self-examine with regard to what had emotionally triggered me to have a mental breakdown. Right now, I am enjoying life, even in the midst of the world and society's chaos, because I am no longer in denial of what or who can negatively trigger my feelings and emotions. One must never downplay what triggers them.

There is a great detriment that one can do to oneself mentally when one is living in denial of their emotional triggers. I am aware that sometimes identifying people, places, and things that serve as mental triggers can become painful. No one wants to be reminded of past negative experiences, but if reverting to them can help the depressed individual deal with their triggers, then it can serve as a positive purpose in the end.

To learn the origin of one's emotional triggers, the depressed individual must continue to be vulnerable and patient. An individual who is working through their emotional triggers should not lose patience with themselves or the mental health specialist when the origin of the triggers does not immediately come to fruition. Once triggers are identified, the depressed individual has a reason and a cause for optimism.

Today, many things in our society affect a depressed individual's emotional state. With the threat of danger and death each day, an individual can be triggered by the local news on television. This may seem minute, but in the world in which we live, anyone can experience emotional trauma.

If an individual who does not suffer from a severe mental illness such as bipolar disorder can become emotionally triggered, then I can only imagine how the depressed individual feels. In the current time we reside in, there is a rise in crime and violence. Many people, including those who are suffering from bipolar disorder, are emotionally triggered with fear and anxiety because of all of the peril all around us.

Who can blame someone who becomes triggered mentally by all of the chaos and turmoil that is threatening our society? Today's world does not offer safety and assurance from experiencing physical, mental, and psychological threats. It is because of these potential threats that many are triggered easily and often. Because of the ongoing danger in the world, it is understandable why many people deal with worry and anxiety.

Unfortunately, I believe that emotional triggers from the world and environment will continue to affect millions. Now I am not at all pessimistic, but I realize how the world is always influencing individuals to become emotionally unstable. When a depressed individual overcomes the emotional triggers of this present world and society, that individual should be commended.

In my opinion, one cannot journey through this sometimes-difficult life when one is constantly triggered. No individual can endure being mentally challenged by triggers while striving to remain emotionally well and stable. Depressed individuals must do their best not to succumb to the triggers of this world.

Mastery of one's emotional triggers can occur. It can become a bit of a challenge, considering the perilous times in which we live. This society is filled with millions of people who are on the verge of psychological illness.

Each individual diagnosed with bipolar disorder will not experience the same triggers simultaneously. Every emotional trigger is unique because we all have different experiences, although we might share the same mental condition. Regardless of how various experiences in life might set off triggers, these emotional threats to one's mental stability are common to all who are living with bipolar disorder.

The key to consistency in coping and living with this severe psychological condition is to recognize and identify those things in life that can potentially affect your emotional and psychological state. To overcome and live successfully with this unpredictable mental condition, the depressed individual must learn about what contributes to their emotional stress. If an individual living with bipolar disorder cannot fathom the things in life that serve as emotional triggers, then their negative emotions will persist.

An individual's emotional triggers can have a plethora of power in the depressed individual's life. These unwanted mental threats must be confronted with bravery and perseverance. Individuals who are emotionally affected by triggers should not become discouraged when triggers are prevalent.

I believe that one can work through one's triggers. The individual who is battling emotional triggers should progress through them gradually, not hastily. When one has a patient approach to anything, this approach will pay off in the end.

Do not become hard on yourself when triggers are not resolved right away. Sometimes, issues and problems in life require that the individual slowly walks through them. Dealing with emotional triggers is no different.

Enduring pain and discomfort is not what many people would prefer to experience in life. Instead, some decide to avoid it at all costs. I wholeheartedly understand why and how the avoidance of stressful issues is desired.

No one in their right frame of mind would like to rehash painful memories. For depressed individuals to release their triggered emotions, they have to express them through intense therapeutic sessions. A viable and reliable psychiatrist with years of experience will not allow an individual with deep emotional triggers to figure out the source of their triggers without their guidance.

Facing today's world is difficult. Many negative situations and occurrences can potentially be encountered each day. If an individual is not emotionally triggered by something, then that individual is not a living and breathing human being. Those who have the challenge of living with bipolar disorder cannot remain emotionally triggered continually if they plan to live victoriously despite it.

Honesty with oneself, as well as with the doctor or therapist, is what is needed to combat and defeat emotional triggers. If one can develop an honest approach to the mental threats they face daily, then the individual can pinpoint the origin of their emotional agony. As we live each day, there is always the potential for someone to experience psychological turmoil.

As I previously stated, it does not do any good to a depressed individual to live in suppression and denial. Choosing to live in utter denial will essentially hurt the individual mentally affected by emotional triggers. Honesty is always the best policy to have when facing anything challenging in life.

Triggers can become difficult to bear, but they do not have to be. I am speaking from experience. When it comes to the uphill battle for mental wellness, properly addressing triggers through counseling and therapy can significantly improve an individual's mental state. The goal for any individual who is struggling with bipolar disorder is to not allow their triggers to inflict harm and pain on themselves as well as on others.

In this chapter, I have tried to discuss the importance of understanding and identifying the people, places, and things that can become mental and emotional stressors and triggers. Some cannot avoid triggers and stressors. For example, an individual who is triggered by other individuals at their workplace or at school can potentially have a difficult time coping with and dealing with the people and things that might stress them.

The individual who is in that stressful position must somehow learn how to go through day-to-day activities while being consistently triggered. Of course, I cannot tell a fellow depressed individual how to react and respond in that unfavorable situation, but this is why talking to a licensed, board-certified psychiatrist is extremely imperative. It requires an enormous amount of commitment and dedication for an individual affected by and living with bipolar disorder to patiently sit through session after session of therapy trying to figure out how to react to emotional triggers.

One thing that I do know about how to react responsibly when triggered is to not react in outward anger or disgust. Responding with a calm demeanor without becoming extremely emotional can be difficult for anyone, but it is something that the individual must do to avoid a toxic situation. There are tools that any individual, including bearers of bipolar disorder, can practice when they are "emotionally charged up."

Sure, it is easy for someone to say to someone, "Do not become emotionally triggered." While in the heat of becoming triggered, the depressed individual must ask themselves, "Is this individual or situation worth me getting emotional and upset over?" Some do not realize how power is given to the people, places, or things that cause the individual to react angrily and emotionally. Identifying and honestly recognizing who or what is an emotional trigger gives the individual the power to not respond negatively.

Chapter 3

Fight the Bipolar Battle
One Day at a Time

For the individual diagnosed with bipolar disorder, living each day in mental wellness can become a daily struggle. With this world and society's decline, it is not easy to have consistency when it comes to one's mental health. I optimistically believe that a depressed individual can become successful in the bipolar battle.

The battle to remain mentally stable is a long one. This particular mental disorder has as many highs as it has lows. Life can become extremely difficult to bear at times, and this is why it is imperative that the individual mentally affected by bipolar disorder develop a positive outlook.

Every depressed person must be willing to fight for their mental wholeness. In this chaotic world in which we live, having an optimistic perspective on life can elude any individual, regardless of their mental status. As an individual who has fought the battle and successfully overcome and coped with bipolar disorder for many years, the only way I come out on the positive side of the mental disease is by living life day-to-day.

An individual coping with bipolar disorder must take each minute and hour as it comes. When the depressed individual can live each day one moment at a time, the mental illness can potentially have less of an effect. Now I am not in any way stating that an individual who is coping with this psychiatric condition is all of a sudden able to successfully fight the bipolar battle when they choose to fight it daily.

With regard to any type of illness, success in overcoming and defeating it does not occur immediately. I must admit that my personal battle with bipolar disorder was not initially triumphant. There were numerous days that I struggled with remaining consistent mentally.

My battle with bipolar disorder was becoming an uncontrollable struggle. One day, it dawned on me that the battle over my mental health and wellness could only improve when I changed my perspective and viewpoint with regard to this psychiatric disorder. From the time that I attacked the illness with an optimistic day-to-day attitude and mindset, I commenced seeing results in my own mental behavior.

Soon, others in my life began to see that I was serious about overcoming my mental struggle with bipolar disorder. If any individual desires to overcome anything in life, that individual must not view it as something bigger than life itself. Bipolar disorder, although significant, should not become dominant in the depressed individual's life.

Sure, this mental condition is serious, and in many cases, it is severe. Some severe cases of bipolar disorder are difficult to experience for the individual suffering from it and for those who are closest to them. The battle over an individual's mental stability can, at times, be a "rocky one."

No individual battling the struggle over bipolar disorder can fight it by themselves. A supportive friend or loved one must also be willing to battle the mental condition. In due time, the battle over this psychiatric disease is most successfully fought when the depressed individual can battle it initially in the short term.

As mere humans, we like to anticipate the long-term effect of any goal that we set out to accomplish. One goal that every individual who is battling this sometimes debilitating mental illness has is to consistently remain mentally well. I cannot emphasize enough how my battle with bipolar disorder was not overcome and combated while striving to anticipate the long-term effect.

The battle with bipolar disorder commenced for me when I was still in my teens. In hindsight, how I was initially diagnosed when I was so young could have been a blessing. When many of us are young, we do not envision how our lives will be twenty to thirty years from now.

If one lives long enough, that individual will soon discover that plans change. In most cases, they (plans) do not remain the same. After I was initially diagnosed with bipolar disorder, I never considered how there would be times when I would have to alter certain plans and goals to fight for my mental stability.

As we are currently aware, life is extremely unpredictable. One does not know what challenge, life-altering issue, or problem one will encounter within a given day. No one wakes up in the morning anticipating a battle.

Though one cannot always predict when one will face daily struggles, they also cannot be avoided. Mental conditions, such as bipolar disorder, are usually within the depressed individual's family history. But there are some instances in which the individual affected by the condition cannot help but become intertwined in the mental struggle.

In my opinion, any individual can be thrust into a battle over their mental health. Think about the millions of people who become so consumed with life that they inadvertently neglect the need for their minds to rest. It is because of many individuals' need to survive life by trying to acquire its basic necessities that many do not understand the need for peace of mind.

Some make matters worse by drinking alcohol and consuming other mood-altering and chemical substances that affect the brain. Bipolar disorder is just as much a brain disorder as it is a mood disorder. Chemical imbalances can come as a result of an individual's consumption of alcohol and mind-altering drugs.

Regardless of how and why an individual becomes diagnosed with bipolar disorder, once diagnosed, the individual is in one of the most significant battles in life that they will ever have to face or encounter. A depressed individual must never be defeated by what is stated in their given prognosis. The battle over one's mental health is never won when the individual succumbs to what is initially revealed by a doctor or therapist.

One must never look too far ahead when battling bipolar disorder. Instead, the depressed individual should battle the illness with bravery and courage. Battling this disease daily requires a plethora of perseverance.

Approaching this mental disorder with a day-to-day mindset essentially helped me personally recover from it. I am cognizant of the fact that there is currently no cure for this psychological condition. Each day that a depressed individual has a chance to live, that individual has a chance of recovery.

We all have something in life that we are battling or recovering from. No individual coping with and living with bipolar disorder should feel frustrated when the recovery becomes difficult. In fact, any type of recovery is never simple and easy, and this is why a day-to-day approach is extremely beneficial.

Recovery is typically gradual. Becoming consistent in the battle with bipolar disorder can occur when the affected individual views the battle as such. There is a process that every individual must experience when recovering from this particular psychological illness.

For example, the depressed individual has to take their prescribed medicine each day. Some who suffer from bipolar disorder do not view the taking of prescribed psychotropic medicine as a way to battle and recover from the psychological illness. I personally believe that consistency in taking the prescribed medicine is one of the key components in fighting bipolar disorder.

When depressed individuals miss their daily dosage of medicine, it lessens their chance of recovery and victory over the disorder. For some, taking medicine can be viewed as a negative, but those who are opposed to taking it do not realize how medicine can strengthen the affected individual's mind over time. A mind that becomes strong is reliable.

To have a mind free from manic or depressive episodes, the individual who is psychologically affected must participate in the process of consuming the psychotropic drugs, along with regular counseling and doctor's visits, to have a chance for mental victory over bipolar disorder. The reason some are not successful in the bipolar battle is that many do not desire to see the whole process through. Individuals who suffer from bipolar disorder do not magically become better.

As an individual who believes in the power of faith, I know that this is also a crucial factor in winning the bipolar fight. An individual who is bipolar must believe that he or she will eventually become well enough to combat and overcome it. What ultimately matters in one's fight over this severe psychological condition is the individual's mind and will.

Just like an individual can have the will to live, a depressed individual must also have the will to battle. After an individual suffering from the illness experiences various signs and symptoms of the disorder, I can understand why it can be easy for the individual to lose hope and surrender. Those who are truly resilient and fighters in life will continue to focus on their long battle of recovery each day instead of living in a state of agony and defeat.

Building successful days one day at a time can help the bearer of the disorder develop more mental patience. It can become extremely difficult to have patience when your mind and thoughts are racing. The last thing that a depressed individual who is full of anxiety and mania wants to hear is patience.

I wholeheartedly believe that the battle against bipolar disorder is won when the depressed individual can remain calm and not act in haste. Psychotropic drugs are prescribed to help the bearer of the mental disease acquire mental balance. I can recall, as an individual who is a bipolar patient, times when I did not believe that taking medicine each day for a substantial amount of time would basically help me in the long run.

For over ten years, I have been blessed enough to continue winning the daily battle over this mental disorder. During those years of successfully coping with the psychological illness, my perception and perspective of the condition drastically changed. I began to consider how taking medicine daily is not a sign of weakness but a contributing factor to prolonged success in this daily battle, along with remaining consistent in my mental health and wellness.

Some naively think that the battle over bipolar disorder is won when the individual does not have to take medicine. Unfortunately, many who are bearers of this psychological illness share that same mindset. If an individual who is affected by this condition can understand and realize how taking medicine each day does contribute to successfully battling the illness, then I would hope that the individual can do what it requires to take that initiative.

There was a time when I was losing the mental battle with this psychological disorder. Regretfully, I contributed to being on the brink of losing the battle over this condition because I did not see how I was hurting myself by not putting in the effort to take the prescribed medicine on time. An individual who is a bearer of bipolar disorder can expect to lose the fight over their mental health when they are not committed to doing what is necessary to remain mentally stable and fit.

Once I started taking the prescribed medicine, I commenced to feel joyous and was back to my old self again. When an individual diagnosed with bipolar disorder reacts to the process of becoming mentally stable with rebelliousness and skepticism, defeat is on the horizon. Defeat from bipolar disorder occurs when the depressed individual is either stagnated in their mental condition or they sadly succumb to the psychological disease.

As an individual who has fought the battle with bipolar disorder for essentially half of my life, I am living proof that an individual who is struggling with a psychological illness can ultimately win the battle. One must realize that the battle with bipolar disorder is never won alone. The process, which includes the daily consumption of psychotropic medicine, intense therapy from a viable, board-certified psychiatrist and/or therapist, and a reliable support system, can help the individual fight a winning battle over a psychological disorder that is not always easily experienced.

Just like any other battle in life, it can become grueling. The battle to remain mentally stable after being afflicted with bipolar disorder can be tough. To make matters worse, our environment is becoming increasingly turbulent and unsafe.

It is not easy to fight one's battle with bipolar disorder when the times in which we live are negative. Mental illness has been at the forefront before our society transitioned from prosperity to now becoming a society affected by economic and financial ruin. The reason I am mentioning the economic decline of our nation is that programs for those who are battling mental disorders, like bipolar disorder, are in great jeopardy.

Many in this nation, as well as all around the world, are in need of support with regard to their mental wellness. Individuals who are affected by bipolar disorder must have others who are willing to roll up their sleeves and help them with the fight against this mental disease day by day. Although the world is chaotic and difficult, the depressed individual should strive to always live for tomorrow.

I will not sugarcoat the fact that it is a challenge to remain present in the bipolar battle. Without sufficient support, the battle to successfully cope with bipolar disorder can potentially be lost. Fighting this never-ending battle for one's mind does not have to end in defeat and sadness.

When a depressed individual is blessed enough to wake up in the morning, the individual is a winner. Having a positive support system can lead an individual who bears the condition on the road to victory and success. Today, as a result of many businesses and practices going to virtual appointments because of this terrible pandemic, bipolar individuals cannot heavily rely upon visiting support groups in person.

This is why immediate family members are vital in the depressed individual's fight to remain consistent mentally. I am not stating that support for the individual battling this severe mental disorder is running scarce, but what I am saying is that individuals who are advocates for individuals who are affected by bipolar disorder can also be experiencing the lingering effects of decreasing funds and support from programs for those who suffer from any type of mental illness.

Some people dealing with and coping with bipolar disorder each day are at a disadvantage. One reason a depressed individual can be in an unfavorable position is that the world as we know it is currently forming into a world of destruction and confusion. An individual who is battling bipolar disorder daily may not have any hope that their condition will eventually improve and change for the better because society is crumbling before their very eyes.

If one cannot envision future hope for the world and society in which they live, then their attitude and mindset will also be negatively affected. A mindset of negativity will have the depressed individual at their wit's end, trying to overcome a mental disorder that is predicated on their thoughts and feelings. The fight over one's mental health requires that the bearer develop the mental fortitude to mentally face it in the daily grind of life.

Consistency in positive thoughts is the goal for the individual affected by bipolar disorder. Positive thoughts are not always easy to come by. Thoughts of optimism are always threatened by the negative events and occurrences that any individual can encounter daily.

How can one who is suffering from bipolar disorder remain positive when the world is far from it? As an individual who has battled and is currently winning the fight over bipolar disorder, I suggest that the depressed individual develops continuous optimism when one becomes committed and motivated to remain mentally healthy. I believe that when any individual is determined and motivated to accomplish any goal of victory over a stumbling block in life, it can definitely become a reality. Yes, I personally view bipolar disorder as a derailment from happiness and joy.

An individual who is not joyous in their life as a result of being afflicted with this psychological condition is not living in victory. This is the very reason the depressed individual must make it their goal to become motivated and not allow the illness to determine their mood. Some people experience depression when the weather outside is dark and gloomy.

I believe that when the battle is won each day over bipolar disorder, the mood of the depressed individual is balanced and positive, regardless of any external factors that may be present. In my opinion, this positive mood and mindset can be achieved, but it does not happen immediately. Our minds and hearts have to be cleansed from the situations and circumstances that could have contributed to becoming mentally triggered in the past.

One cannot become victorious in their battle over psychological illness by replaying those negative thoughts that have constantly plagued their mind for so long. The negative thoughts of an individual affected by bipolar disorder must be limited to a minimum. We all have negative thoughts that could creep into our minds on any given day.

With regard to those negative thoughts, one can either listen to them or disregard them by doing something enjoyable and creative. Previously, I stated that psychotropic drugs, therapy, and counseling, as well as a reliable support system, are vital in the depressed individual's daily battle with the disorder. Sure, these people and activities do help the individual fight this mental health battle, but there is more to it than that.

The individual struggling in their battle with bipolar disorder may have all the resources and support to face the battle over their minds head-on, but ultimately, the battle is won and lost with their thoughts from within. If the depressed individual can somehow change their thought process and perception of things in life that could negatively influence their mind, I believe that the individual can have a more positive mood and mindset. What one thinks about each day, internally and mentally, determines whether or not the battle over a consistent mood finally comes into focus.

One can become successful in their struggle with bipolar disorder when they become more mentally focused and aware. Individuals battling bipolar disorder can gain victory over it when they are mentally aware of what they are up against. This mental condition is not the depressed individual's friend.

Bipolar disorder is the bearer's opponent. When the condition is treated patiently and aggressively each day, I believe that, in due time, the disorder can lose its grip on the individual who is currently struggling with it. To cope and fight successfully each day in this mental health battle, depressed individuals must continue to focus on their healing.

Many people talk about how bipolar disorder and other mental health issues are having a negative impact. Instead of focusing on how many are affected by this mental disease, the focus should primarily be on ways to overcome the battle and struggle over it. In other words, the individual afflicted with the mental condition, as well as those who are proponents and advocates of the mentally ill, should battle the illness by discovering ways to inform individuals who are still experiencing the signs and symptoms that there is still hope and encouragement out there.

An individual who is in the midst of bipolar disorder must find positive ways to be encouraged each day. I believe that looking at others who have been able to overcome many adversities in life can help an individual living with and coping with bipolar disorder think to themselves, *If that person can fight and overcome a life-threatening disease by living through it, then I can also do the same with my condition.* Inspiration from others can motivate someone who is having a difficult time enduring an illness to continue to fight despite whatever circumstances result.

I believe that many who are battling bipolar disorder can battle it and eventually cope and live with it. The only way that a depressed individual cannot combat it is when the space in between their ears dares not to fight and battle. Now enduring a fight over one's mind is not for the faint of heart.

It requires the depressed individual to prepare themselves for the potential for mental obstacles. While battling bipolar disorder, there will be times when it may seem as though the individual will not be able to regain their positive attitude and mindset. This is why I can honestly state that overcoming the battle over this psychological illness is a marathon, not a sprint.

Many people are only prepared for the hour-long version of issues and problems in life. What I mean by that statement is that some people naively think that their problems are like television programs that are typically over after the hourly program ends. Life, as well as bipolar disorder, is far from being dealt with and coped with after a relatively short time. Putting in the daily work to become better mentally is what all individuals enduring this mental condition must do to survive.

Is it in you to fight? As an individual who welcomes adversities and challenges, at this stage in my life, I must admit that there was a time when I ran when challenges and mishaps came my way. To any individual who is enduring the challenge of remaining mentally fit, I would like to say to you to keep it going. One should never quit pursuing to become mentally well and whole.

Fighting the battle with bipolar disorder has always been an inward mental battle. Once depressed individuals are mentally whole, they have enough courage and power to face and endure anything that life throws at them. Mental illnesses, such as bipolar disorder, can affect an individual in several negative ways.

One way having bipolar disorder can negatively affect the individual experiencing it is by having an apathetic attitude and mindset. Individuals with that particular mindset do not have any motivation to do what it takes to improve from where they were initially diagnosed. They are content to remain mentally and psychologically stationary.

No one with a lack of interest and concern for their mental health can experience the satisfaction that depressed individuals have when they conquer their "mental demons." To overcome mental health struggles, individuals must have the desire to control their moods and thoughts. There has to be a proactive approach to fighting this severe psychological illness.

Another way bipolar disorder can have negative connotations for depressed individuals is when they are lazy and lethargic mentally. I am not referring to an individual who is tired and in need of sleep and rests from time to time. I believe that a well-rested individual who is a bearer of the condition has the potential to become mentally sharp.

In fact, a well-rested brain is a mentally active one. Many people in the midst of a manic or depressive episode are not experiencing any type of rest, whether it is mental or physical. Those who are in a manic phase are not resting because of the enormous energy that they experience.

As a result of this mental phase, the mind and brain ultimately suffer. On the other end of the spectrum, when an individual is in a relatively depressed state of mind, that individual is also not resting properly. Have you ever heard of the saying, "There is no rest for the weary"? A weary brain is also a tired brain.

Every individual who has battled bipolar disorder cannot fight it when they are always mentally and physically tired. Think about it. World-class fighters never enter the championship battle for the title without resting before the bout.

Fighters are aware that the battle is fought and won when their energy is conserved. With regard to the battle with bipolar disorder, this same concept should also apply. The battle over one's mind is best fought with a rested mind.

Responding positively to the mental health struggle is important for coping with and fighting the bipolar battle. As I stated in the previous chapter, when one's emotional triggers are minimized, the individual who is the bearer of the psychological disorder has a greater chance of success and victory over it. An individual who is mentally struggling can now one day thrive mentally.

In my opinion, my faith in the Creator has helped me tremendously. Just because I have faith in God does not mean that I should negate taking prescribed medicine. Some consider those who take medicine for any serious health condition inferior.

Medicine is vital to improvement, but with bipolar disorder, medicine is just a portion of fighting the daily mental health battle. The depressed individual must continue to work on having a positive self-image. If the sufferer can somehow progress in their mental self-image, then that individual will become better equipped to face the ongoing task and challenge of sustaining stability in their mind and mood.

This daily mental health struggle has to be fought with patience and endurance. One who is afflicted by bipolar disorder cannot successfully defeat it without considering the fact that the progression of time in dealing with and coping with the psychological disorder can be both essential and beneficial. In most cases, this psychological condition is typically treated and controlled when the individual affected by it is mentally stable over time.

During my own battle with bipolar disorder, I did not envision the day that this mental disease would not have the dominion to affect me each day in the way that it once did. Instead of avoiding the battle over my mental health, I learned how to embrace it. How does one get to the point of anticipating the bipolar battle? The individual must acquire the mental confidence from within to not allow their mind to succumb to this mental condition.

We all have to live each day in this world. No one is assured of what the next day will bring. Life should be lived, not just experienced.

Sure, one can experience the devastating impact of bipolar disorder on their lives, but it does not have to remain a negative factor. Every individual who has ever been afflicted with this psychological condition is initially overwhelmed by how difficult it can be at times to remain mentally afloat. When someone is first diagnosed with bipolar disorder, that individual, along with their family members and friends, is not mentally prepared to fight the lifelong mental health battle, which can negatively cause friction in the lives of the bearer as well as those who are closest and dearest to them.

An individual who is not mentally prepared to battle this often-times painful psychological disease will have to endure times of difficulty and adversity. No one can claim victory over bipolar disorder in the midst of mental turmoil and confusion. Victory and success require steadfastness, growth, and eagerness to succeed, and dealing with and coping with this mental condition also encompass those same qualities.

Conflict in one's mind is ultimately the synopsis of mental disorders, such as bipolar disorder. In this life, there is always some sort of conflict formulating. With regard to an individual battling with and coping with this particular psychological disorder, the battle and conflict over their mind can become a daily nemesis.

If you, as a depressed individual, cannot journey through life with at least a laugh and a smile from time to time, then you are currently losing the mental health war. I am cognizant of the fact that the times in which we live are not filled with joy and happiness. A lot in this world and society is threatening the potential of someone experiencing each day with laughter and joy.

Bipolar disorder can steal an individual's will to live and enjoy life. So many in this world and society are being robbed of ever experiencing consistency in their mind and moods because they are wallowing in pity and despair. Just because someone is diagnosed with this mental disease does not mean that their life is over and done with.

An individual who is struggling with their mental health must develop the courage and mental toughness to fight this daily war over their mind and thoughts. When it comes to negative thoughts, the depressed individual does not have to entertain them. The battle over this psychological condition is won and lost by one's thoughts.

If you think that you will win the battle over your mental health, then you must never allow yourself to think otherwise. This mindset of mental confidence and positive visions commences when the individual lives one day at a time. Each person battling the mental conflict of bipolar disorder must never lose sight of winning the war over their mind.

Some might say that to accomplish anything in life, an individual must learn how to take "baby steps." Babies do not all of a sudden have a knack for crawling and walking. They work at doing those functions "little by little."

One day, the baby masters crawling, and before he or she can walk, that baby becomes proficient at crawling. The saying that an individual has to "crawl before they walk" can be adopted in the mindset of an individual who is battling with and dealing with bipolar disorder daily. Before an individual can experience daily consistency in their mind, they have to first acquire the tools and mindset to face this difficult mental challenge.

Acquiring the tools and mindset to fight bipolar disorder does not happen instantly in the life of a bipolar sufferer. One has to work closely with their doctor or therapist to achieve the desired result, which is to first win the battle and then ultimately win the war with the illness. Battles typically pale in comparison to wars.

Because battles are small, they can be more easily resolved. I am not saying that the battle with bipolar disorder can be solved quickly and immediately, because that is just simply untrue. Having the mindset and will to be persistent in one's quest to fight and face the battle each day to remain mentally whole and fit is ultimately a successful battle.

Chapter 4

Envision Overcoming
the Disorder

A person with bipolar disorder does not have to remain in a negative mental state. Though there is no cure for the psychological condition, the individual bearing the disease should remain hopeful. This psychological disorder can only be overcome when the depressed individual has a vision of overcoming it.

I believe that I have successfully coped with bipolar disorder for several years because I had a vision of consistency in my mental wellness. One will not improve mentally if a vision is not established. Individuals who are the most successful in coping with and dealing with this psychological illness are the ones with dreams of mental success.

It does not matter how disappointing their prognosis might be; if the individual has visions of hope, they can thrive even in the midst of a devastating illness. With regard to bipolar disorder, my hope for the depressed individual is that he or she does not remain in the same state of mind. Some people remain stagnant when a doctor reveals bad news to them.

Now I am not saying that an individual who receives negative news from a physician or a doctor should disregard what the expert might reveal or discover about their condition. What I am saying is that an individual should not lose hope that the illness or sickness can gradually improve. There are millions of people in this nation and worldwide who never envision a life of wellness.

I would like to encourage individuals who are struggling with their mental health to strive to envision a day when their mind and mood are balanced. Becoming mentally whole and stable does not come to fruition without vision, hope, and determination. It does not mean that the depressed individual who has a vision of mental stability will overcome the psychological disorder completely, but that individual does not have to live in mental chaos and confusion.

Depressed individuals must somehow envision themselves as prospering mentally. One of the ways in which I was personally able to overcome bipolar disorder is by not referring to myself as an individual who is "bipolar." Instead, the vision that I had for my life that helped me in the past and is currently helping and influencing my mental health progress is envisioning myself as a respectable, normal human being.

With any dream or goal in life, the only way that an individual can accomplish it is through dedication and focus. Yes, I have dedicated my life to viewing myself as a whole and able-bodied person. In the past, I could not have imagined that I would become a writer, let alone write books about how an individual can live successfully in this world despite being diagnosed with a psychological illness.

Individuals who might be struggling mentally can dream big. Some would probably suggest that it is a foolish dream for an individual stricken with a mental condition like bipolar disorder to have an "unattainable goal or dream" of living mentally whole consistently. Every illness, including bipolar disorder, does not have to destroy one's vision for one's life or be a "dream killer" for that person.

Our minds are extremely powerful. It is within the mind that concepts and visions of dreams form. A mind that can dream is a mind that has the potential to become unstoppable.

Many of us do not dare to have a dream, goal, or vision because our thoughts tell us that it is impossible. Someone can tell you that what you may envision for your life will not happen, but only you can decide whether or not you will prove the critics right or wrong.

With regard to goals and dreams, we are our own worst enemies when it comes to fulfilling a vision.

Most individuals who are diagnosed with bipolar disorder will not envision any type of dream or plan. Even if the dream or vision does consist of one day overcoming this severe mental illness, some relinquish their plan of becoming more mentally consistent and stable because they have set their own limitations. Although this world and society are in a state of turmoil, an individual who is mentally affected by bipolar disorder does not have to be.

As long as the depressed individual can maintain a daily routine and regimen of taking the prescribed medications, sleeping adequately, and attending counseling and therapy sessions, there is always the potential to overcome this mental disorder. What gets many individuals who are living with this condition into trouble is that many think that when they become well for a substantial period, they become automatically cured of this illness. Overcoming bipolar disorder does not mean that the depressed individual is void of some semblance of mental strife.

Having dominion over this psychological condition is only acquired when the bearer of the illness uses their mind as a valued part of their body. Once they view their mind as an ally, the vision and goals that they have set to remain mentally stable by overcoming this psychological disease will occur. The goal and vision of sustaining mental consistency that every individual who is coping with and living with bipolar disorder desires must be shared with the affected individual's doctor/therapist as well as the individual's support system.

When I initially envisioned overcoming bipolar disorder, it did not come to fruition immediately. The process of remaining mentally consistent was difficult and trying at first. After some time had elapsed, I commenced to realize how my vision of overcoming bipolar disorder was starting to pay off.

There were times that I thought I would never experience the potential of not being overwhelmed by this mental health struggle. Although it seemed as though the vision that I formulated would elude me, I still had optimism. Sometimes, a vision might seem out of reach, but in actuality, it is closer than one thinks. An individual who is daring enough to formulate a vision of sustainability in mental wellness can also experience a great reward of mental bliss when the vision becomes a reality.

Imagine having continuous days of mental bliss. I believe that it does not become a reality until the mentally affected individual creates a mental vision of wellness. Depressed individuals can and will succeed in coping with bipolar disorder when they are committed and focused on their vision of mental consistency.

As an individual who has developed great faith over time, I have also had the belief that I could one day improve mentally. There were years when I struggled mightily with my mental health. My battle to remain mentally whole and well became an unwanted challenge.

For years, I was always experiencing some kind of psychotic episode. It had gotten to the point that even my psychiatrist and therapist, who I was working with during those difficult times, did not think that my future in life looked promising. I was hospitalized so many times that the staff at the hospital commenced to know me on a first-name basis.

During those years of darkness, I did not envision a successful life. In my opinion, a life of success is when an individual can live with joy and contentment. Bipolar disorder is a mental condition that typically does not equate to a life of favor.

So many individuals who are afflicted with this severe psychological illness do not feel that envisioning a life of mental wellness is necessary. They are just watching life pass them by. In other words, many of the individuals who suffer from bipolar disorder live in total uncertainty.

An individual who is unsure about life will definitely not come up with a vision for it. Those who are mentally affected by bipolar disorder can live a life of assurance and certainty. But before the depressed individual can experience confidence and successful living, they must somehow develop a purpose and a plan.

One's life can drastically improve for the better when they have the vision and the will to defy the odds and overcome life's challenges and mishaps. This mental disease will always have the potential to negatively manifest itself in the life of the sufferer. Individuals who have been successfully coping with bipolar disorder for an enormous amount of time have overcome the triggers and symptoms of the psychological condition.

Faith and belief in one's ability to experience consistency in mental wellness do not occur without a mental vision. Once someone is diagnosed with bipolar disorder, it is extremely difficult to have a positive mental perception of themselves. An individual who is initially a receiver of the bad news of their mental condition is not automatically thinking about how they will become consistent mentally.

Instead, they are immediately questioning how they will experience mental relief. The question that an individual who is thinking about relief from this devastating psychiatric illness has is, "When will this mental nightmare end?" It is during that time that a vision or goal for prolonged mental stability is not even a consideration. Depressed individuals will discover their vision of overcoming bipolar disorder when they become frustrated and tired of always being psychologically ill.

Excelling in life is what many try to envision. In these modern times, some who are diagnosed with bipolar disorder are quietly living successful and inspired lives. With the threat of pestilence and other issues affecting the world and society, I hope that those who are diagnosed as "bipolar" do not regress or lose sight of remaining mentally stable.

It is extremely imperative that an individual who is mentally affected by bipolar disorder continue to envision consistency in their mind and mood. Those who have developed mental consistency are generally productive members of society. Individuals who suffer from the disorder should not accept the negative labels and stigma that society places on them.

No depressed individual should abandon their dreams and visions because of what others may perceive as their vision. An individual who is afflicted with bipolar illness must not live their life at the expense of others. What truly counts in their lives is how they can bring their visions and dreams to fruition.

With regard to dreams and visions, they are not always easily obtained. We, as mere human beings, have to decide between relinquishing the vision we have for our life or trying to hold onto it in some way. Overcoming bipolar disorder is not only reserved for becoming mentally whole and balanced.

It means that the individual can still have the same goals, visions, and dreams as others who are not affected by mental illness. Some people who are coping with bipolar disorder are afraid to have a vision of any kind or a dream. Because individuals, especially some depressed individuals, experience a lack of support and motivation to dream and have a vision of how they would like their lives to go, some put their visions aside or on the backburner.

The way that an individual who is affected by bipolar disorder can overcome the psychological condition is by not setting limits on their dreams or visions. One might say, "I cannot dream that vision or goal because I am bipolar." Excuses are sadly what many who are afflicted with this mental disease do to themselves because they do not have the confidence to dream big dreams and bring that vision about.

I believe that it is within the realm of any individual who suffers from this psychological disorder to set out plans and visions for their life. Sure, some situations and scenarios require that the dream or vision that they set out to accomplish change. When this occurs, the individual should not remain fixated on the original plan.

In this life, nothing remains the same. This also applies to plans and visions. Once the depressed individual can overcome and deal successfully with bipolar disorder, they must also acquire the ability to adopt another dream and vision when their plans have to move in another direction.

Happiness is what many of us strive for. With regard to living with bipolar disorder, some are not experiencing the joy of life. It is difficult to enjoy life when the illness is negatively affecting their minds.

As the unlikeliest individual to have joy and happiness despite my past struggles with the disorder, I have been able to experience the joy of living because I viewed myself as an individual who has overcome the mental health battle. I reiterate that I may not be fully cured of the psychological condition, but I am coping with it just fine. The reason I can confidently state that I am successfully battling bipolar disorder is that I had a vision of mental success.

August 2010 was the last time that I was hospitalized because of mental illness. At that time, I was struggling mentally. Now do not mistake me; I was taking the medicine that was prescribed, but the medicine that I was taking at the time was not the right fit for me.

Because the psychotropic medicine did not work, I experienced the signs and symptoms of the mental disorder. After being mentally stable with the right prescribed medicine, my psychological condition drastically improved. Once I regained my mental health, I decided that I would do everything in my power to remain consistent in my mood and mind.

It was through mental imagery that I began to envision becoming mentally stable not only for one day but also for the succeeding years to come. In the years preceding my vision of consistency in mental wellness, I did not have any plan on how to mentally remain whole continuously. Naively, I thought that only taking the prescribed medicine would suffice.

If any depressed individual has a chance of mental consistency for the duration of their life, they must envision themselves mentally well every day. There is no known formula to sustain consistency in mental wellness other than doing the things suggested and advised by a doctor/therapist. An individual who is motivated and determined to realize a vision is not only a dreamer but also one who makes things happen.

A goal or a vision is only potential. Many people in this world initially start the process of setting up a plan to realize a dream, but somehow along the way, plans sometimes go awry. One does not have to wish that one can remain mentally stable because it does not have to be a dream.

An individual who is afflicted with bipolar disorder does not have to continue to live in mental turmoil and agony. Sure, some may suggest that an individual who is once diagnosed as bipolar should remain in the same mental state upon diagnosis. When an individual who is mentally affected by bipolar disorder realizes how the disease can be treated and coped with successfully each day, they will soon understand that they have more than just the potential to overcome the psychological disorder and that they can come up with a vision and plan to attack and combat it.

Each individual who desires to overcome this mental condition will not be successful in winning the mental battle without courage and faith. It takes faith to make up one's mind that this psychological disease will not rule their whole life. Sadly, some are at the mercy of this psychological disorder.

It requires courage to do what is needed to remain mentally well. Although the stigma of being diagnosed with bipolar disorder is not as negative as it once was, there is still an uphill battle for many who are afflicted with it in society. When I turn on the local and national news, it is not uncommon for me to hear the news of a so-called crazed individual who has committed acts of violence being diagnosed at some point in their life with some particular mental illness.

I cannot personally speak for all who are afflicted with some sort of mental condition, but I know that the majority of the mentally ill are not crazed criminals. Some are just having a mental struggle, and that does not make the depressed individual a bad person. Listening to others' negative opinions can sometimes affect an individual battling a psychological condition.

Personally, I love to see and hear about individuals with bipolar disorder who are doing well mentally. I believe that not only do psychiatric drugs, therapy, and a reliable support system help depressed individuals overcome the psychological disorder, but also consistency in their internal and mental thought processes can make a world of difference in their mood and behavior. Once consistency in their mood and thoughts is accomplished, they can also envision overcoming it.

Most visions that many individuals have in this life are personal. During the time that I envisioned a life of mental consistency, I did not discuss it with my doctor or members of my support system. I kept this plan and goal to overcome bipolar disorder to myself.

As an individual who has succeeded in accomplishing what I set out to do, I did not want anyone to deter me or talk me out of my vision of sustaining years of mental stability. Of course, there were times that I could have given in to the emotional triggers that could have potentially set me back on my mental wellness and wholeness journey, but I refused to allow my emotional triggers to have that power over me. A depressed individual who does not yield to the negative traumas of the past can still cope successfully with bipolar disorder and experience a bright future.

We would all like to experience mental comfort. Because there is so much chaos and turmoil each day, any individual's quest to acquire peace of mind and a life of joy and peace that can elude many is threatened. A sufferer of bipolar disorder can envision a life of mental comfort when the process of overcoming the disorder is envisioned and embedded within the individual.

This particular psychological condition can be overcome. The key to an individual who is mentally affected by the disease overcoming it is knowledge of the disorder and confidence. When a depressed individual has either a manic or depressive episode, the last thing that they may be thinking about is how they will eventually be victorious over the illness.

A depressed individual thinks about survival and mental relief while in the midst of a psychotic episode. In my opinion, there are not too many individuals who discuss and talk about how bipolar disorder does not have to ruin their lives. I personally feel that I understand how easy it is for an individual experiencing a psychological condition to get down on themselves.

If you, the reader, or someone you love is having a difficult time with this psychological illness, I believe that there is always hope. An individual who is battling a mental disease must learn how to persevere through psychotic episodes that they may experience. One can overcome the disorder despite the depressed individual's numerous mental breakdowns.

In my own experience with bipolar disorder, I have experienced a few psychotic episodes. When I was experiencing those mental health conflicts, my mindset was not at all focused on how I could eventually move past that mental battle. My mental state was not at all strong enough during that time to combat and face this psychological illness that could have a negative influence on someone.

It took several years of battling bipolar disorder before I became mentally able to exercise my "mental demons." No individual who suffers from bipolar disorder can effectively cope and successfully overcome it over time without following and listening to what a board-certified and licensed psychiatrist/therapist advises. Most mental health professionals and experts would love to share in their patient's/client's overall mental improvement.

Doctors and mental health professionals who can support their patients' vision of mental consistency should be commended. Depressed individuals who experience support from their psychiatrist are better equipped to consistently overcome this sometimes unpredictable mental illness. Familiarity and comfort are essential to the mentally affected individual's vision of remaining mentally well.

For instance, any individual who feels uncomfortable doing anything in life will not have a particular desire to do that activity because it makes them feel uneasy. They will avoid that uneasy feeling at all costs. Becoming comfortable and familiar with one's doctor/therapist, as well as oneself, plays a vital role in their vision and goal of achieving mental stability and success.

Individuals who experience prolonged familiarity and comfort can essentially thrive mentally. First, to enjoy mental comfort and success, depressed individuals may experience challenging times with regard to their mental health. Those who persevere and do not give up on themselves have a tremendous chance of realizing their plan and vision of successfully combating their mental illness.

Thriving in one's mental health can become challenging, given the uncertain times in which we live. Currently, bipolar disorder affects approximately 5.7 million Americans. It affects nearly fifty-one million people worldwide.

The highest number of individuals affected by this psychological illness is in the United States. We, as a nation, have an enormous mental health crisis on our hands. With the viral threat and other issues and problems that are plaguing our country and society, the topic of mental health is becoming more prevalent and is also a health issue that no one can afford to avoid.

Because mental health disorders, such as bipolar disorder, are becoming more widespread, some people do not envision how any individual dealing with and coping with this severe mental condition can even think about having the audacity to try to successfully combat it and have a vision of winning the bipolar battle. Just like any other health condition, bipolar disorder does not have to be a lifelong liability for the affected individual. In previous years, an individual battling any kind of mental illness was not assured of success in life.

Unfortunately, many decades ago, there were not enough examples of people who were successfully living with bipolar disorder or manic depression, which was the name mental disorder was previously referred to as. As I stated in the book entitled *Overcoming Bipolar Disorder: Defying the Odds*, today, some people we see on our television and movie screens and hear on the radio, along with athletes and politicians, are battling bipolar disorder daily. Each individual struggling with bipolar disorder should never lose hope and patience that they, too, can live lives of infinite possibilities despite having a mental condition.

In this country, we love stories of people who have overcome all kinds of adversities and challenges. Bipolar disorder will always have the potential to pose a challenge or risk to anyone who has ever been diagnosed with the psychological illness. No individual who bears the condition can honestly say to themselves that they will never experience another emotional trigger or psychotic episode.

I believe more than anything that one's mental health must always have precedence and be an individual's top priority. Now overall health and wellness are also extremely important, but an individual's mind gives them the vision and plan to take the necessary precautions to prepare for their overall wellness. One who has great mental health is an individual who can live life freely and uninhibited.

Worry and anxiety over one's mental health are what many in our nation and society are dealing with and experiencing every day. An individual who is constantly worried about their mental health will also have a difficult time with regard to how to overcome their mental health crises and struggles. A mind free from all of the potential mental stress that bipolar disorder produces is also a mind that envisions becoming both stress- and mentally-free.

Recovery from a psychological condition can be obtained. It is not a question of whether an individual can ultimately recover; it is a question of whether or not the recovery from the mental illness will last. My hope for any individual who is experiencing a mental health crisis because of bipolar disorder is that they never lose hope and that the mental disease can be overcome.

The terrible reality with regard to bipolar disorder and other mental illnesses is that they are not easy to recover from for a prolonged time. Because of the uncertainty of how the psychotropic medicine will become effective and the potential for being emotionally triggered, it may seem as though recovering and overcoming the mental condition will never happen. When it comes to remaining mentally stable for a substantial amount of time, it may seem unheard of to some.

Consistency in mental wellness will typically translate to successfully overcoming this psychological illness. In my experience with continuous success with bipolar disorder, I do not think about my previous episodes. I cannot comment on others' experiences with regard to their episodes, but I firmly believe that just because someone has experienced an emotional trigger or mental episode in the past does not mean that they should cease envisioning a life of mental health success.

Overcoming bipolar disorder will not happen for the depressed individual unless they develop the attitude and mindset to envision prolonged success over their mental disorder. Living with a psychological condition does not have to be detrimental. For bipolar disorder not to negatively affect an individual for their entire life, the depressed individual must somehow minimize the illness's effect.

The bearer of the psychological disease essentially decreases the disease's psychological effect on them when they view it as an illness that can be treated and controlled. As someone who has lost some mental battles at times with this mental disease, I am living and breathing proof that bipolar disorder, when treated with the right psychotropic medication and a positive mental outlook and perception, does not have to wreak havoc in the life of the illness's bearer. There is always the potential for becoming ill because of bipolar disorder, and that is why many do not discuss how the mental disorder can potentially become a nonfactor in a sufferer's life once they are mentally balanced and stabilized.

In my opinion, a bipolar individual must become cautiously optimistic. They should not live with overconfidence and arrogance when they have overcome bipolar disorder. Always remember that when the symptoms of the illness are treated and kept relatively tamed, one should continue to do the same things they did in managing the psychological sickness.

Health is just as important as living and breathing. Our mental health is also crucial. Without relatively good mental health, an individual cannot live a life of quality and value.

An individual who has developed a vision of overcoming bipolar disorder can see their goal of good mental health come to fruition. Most visions of success, especially with regard to winning the battle over this mental disorder, are not as easy as one may think. There are a plethora of hardships that depressed individuals may experience before they can overcome this mental adversity.

Bipolar disorder will always have those affected wondering if they can really and truly get over their psychological disease. Getting over bipolar disorder does not mean that the bearer of the condition is suddenly and magically cured. What getting over the disorder means, in my opinion, is that the mental disease is less of a factor and a mental fixture in the mind of the depressed person.

It is unrealistic to think that, with the snap of a finger, bipolar disorder will all of a sudden disappear. Once an individual is diagnosed with a mental condition, it becomes a part of their life for as long as they are blessed enough to live on this earth. In other words, the illness is always embedded in their minds.

I believe that any individual who is ever diagnosed with bipolar disorder can successfully overcome it when they are open and receptive to doing what it takes to remain mentally stable. Some sufferers of bipolar disorder are stubborn. They will only do what they deem best in trying to overcome the mental disease.

This is the wrong attitude and mindset to have when trying to overcome any health crisis or issue, let alone bipolar disorder. One has to stay on course in their daily regimen and routine to have a chance of becoming successful with this mental health condition. Though the path to mental bliss is challenging at times, once it is acquired, there is a deep level of satisfaction that the individual will experience.

Envisioning a plan or goal in life is what every individual should do. With regard to overcoming this severe psychological disorder, there is no reason an individual should not set a goal of eventually putting the disease behind them. The individual who leaves the illness behind is still affected by it, but the illness no longer has a firm grip on their mind.

A depressed person always has an option: either they disregard the advice of a competent and reliable psychiatrist/therapist when striving to overcome their psychological disorder or wallow on the path of mental destruction. Those who are coping with and living with bipolar disorder have a choice about whether or not they want to fight for their mental health. Prolonged mental bliss cannot become a reality or be accomplished without formulating a positive mental vision of finally overcoming mental anguish.

Chapter 5

Focus on the Positive Things in Life

With the state of this world and society, there is not much that one can become positive about. An individual living with bipolar disorder must strive to discover what is positive in this world. It is imperative that a depressed individual develop a positive attitude and mindset when coping with this psychological illness.

I am cognizant of the fact that it is difficult to manage bipolar disorder when chaos and destruction are way too prevalent. Some people experiencing mental conditions may feel as though there is no hope for the future. Once anyone has that mindset, it becomes difficult to have a positive one.

My suggestion to the individual who is vigorously battling the mental disease is to find something in life that they feel good about. Also, they should try to do activities that they enjoy. If a mentally affected individual can do those things, then I am certain that their mood will change for the better.

We are all journeying through this difficult life, striving to find peace and love. For the bipolar individual, I hope that they have some kind of support. Support can come in many forms.

The world in which we live is made up of billions of people. One who is coping with bipolar disorder must at least have one good and supportive friend if the individual is not fortunate enough to have support from a family member. In a generally cruel and unkind world, this is a positive thing a depressed individual can rely upon.

Sadly, some do not have any support from anyone. Sure, one may not have other individuals around physically who can cheer them on in this mental health battle, but there is always someone within the spiritual realm from whom they should seek support. I am talking about the Creator, the Heavenly Father, Who is a positive influence in any individual's life.

Focusing on God will always result in a positive mental health state. Initially, when any individual is trying to develop a spiritual relationship with the Almighty, there will probably be difficult times. Those who seek spiritual growth may not discover the positive benefits of life when they are initially walking with God. Our Heavenly Father, as well as His Son, Jesus Christ, can always do the impossible.

When my battle with bipolar disorder became extremely challenging, I had to somehow focus on what in this life is good and positive. Ultimately, I found someone who was there for me even in the midst of my mental turmoil and agony from this psychological health battle. That someone, with whom I realized was always there for me despite my struggles with bipolar disorder, was none other than the Creator of life and the entire world and universe—God.

It is the Creator, Himself, to whom every individual facing any type of health concern must turn to discover a positive perspective when it comes to life's adversities. I am aware of how difficult it is trying it is to experience positive things in life when one's mood is not in a positive state. Those who are afflicted and living with bipolar disorder can live successfully with it if they focus on positive things in life, which can influence them to have a positive attitude.

Positive dreams and goals will always prove beneficial to the individual affected by this mental condition. When dreams and goals are positively formulated, it can result in an individual becoming mentally stimulated. A mentally stimulated mind has a clear and alert mind.

The goal for every individual who is in the midst of a mental battle is mental clarity. Once depressed individuals regain a clear mind, they will eventually be able to focus their minds on positive things in life. It is imperative that an individual struggling with their mood and thoughts revert to those positive memories of the past to overcome the negative memories resulting from bipolar disorder.

As someone who has overcome the mental disorder thus far, I would not have been able to do so without focusing on the positive things that I could accomplish in life. Just because an individual may currently have negative issues and problems that stem from this psychological disease does not mean that they do not have someone or something positive in their life.

I wholeheartedly believe that we can all find something positive and worthwhile in our lives. Some may think that those positive things do not exist. If one searches deep within, there is always something positive that one can discover.

In this life, there are always positive and negative situations and circumstances. Though some may experience more negative events and occurrences than positive ones in their lives, this does not mean that the positive events are null and void. I would like to encourage those depressed individuals who do not have a positive goal, dream, or vision because of this psychological illness to endure the challenge and adversity because, if you do, you will eventually realize that you do not have to look further than yourself for positive inspiration.

Do not mistake me. A depressed individual should not become arrogant or self-centered when drawing inspiration from themselves. The Creator and His Son must be the prime sources of positive inspiration in one's life.

There is always something positive that every individual can learn about the Almighty, about life, and about themselves. This is why we, those individuals with bipolar disorders in particular, must fill our minds with all of the positive things in life that we can find. Our minds should not be bombarded with continuous negativity, chaos, and confusion.

When this occurs, there is a greater chance that the individual affected by the psychological disease will succumb to negativity. Acquiring a positive attitude and mindset is not as simple as desiring it. Because the world in which we live is increasingly becoming negatively polluted, it is a realistic struggle for any individual, including those who suffer from mental and mood disorders, to have a prolonged focus on the few positive things that are left in this world and society.

Thoughts are typically influenced by what we see and hear. This is why an individual battling this severe mental and mood disorder learns the importance of positive stimuli. We are all stimulated by a plethora of things in life, whether they are positive or negative.

If an individual who is mentally affected by bipolar disorder could somehow become positively stimulated, then that individual could potentially develop consistency in positive thoughts. When an individual's mind is edified with positive stimuli, the mind and brain become positively affected by them. Each individual living in this world feeds his or her brain and mind with something.

For example, a depressed individual who constantly watches violence and horror movies is feeding their mind with negative stimuli. Sometimes, an individual who watches such horrific programs is oblivious that what they hear and see can negatively affect their mind. To make matters worse, an individual does not have to watch a violent or terrible horror movie because the negative stimuli reported each day on the news can contribute to their feelings of mental anguish and discomfort.

For me, I enjoy focusing on God and religion. Religion and faith can be positive stimuli in an individual's mind. Reading and meditating on the scriptures in the Bible have a way of positively affecting an individual's mood and perception.

In my opinion, focusing on the Word of God has a calming effect when anxiety and depression try to "rear their ugly heads." An individual who is coping with bipolar disorder either must discover a positive activity or continue to remain in the same negative and stagnant state. Exercising is an activity that we must all do to remain physically fit, but this activity also has a positive effect on our mood and brain.

This activity should not be dreaded, particularly when it comes to individuals who are suffering from bipolar disorder. Some do not realize that exercising is the one "positive medicine" that does not have to be prescribed. Any individual can focus on this positive activity at their own leisure.

The mental benefit of exercising far outweighs the physical benefits. Exercise helps the individual become mentally engaged. Earlier, I discussed how the mind responds to positive stimuli, and exercising provides that.

Exercise is one of the positive things in life that does not require an enormous amount of mental ability. Nothing is mind-altering about walking or running around the neighborhood or inside the friendly confines of one's home on a safe and effective exercise treadmill. Becoming mentally fit from exercising is both positive and fun, and an individual who is both physically and mentally fit does not have any room to be influenced by negative stimuli.

These perilous times in which we live are a difficult challenge for many. If the times that we are currently residing in are challenging for individuals without a psychological mishap, then imagine how difficult it can be for those who are affected by bipolar disorder. Now more than ever, depressed individuals are likely to experience either manic or depressive episodes because of all the traumatic events and occurrences that essentially affect their mental health.

Realistically, an individual who is mentally affected by bipolar disorder is not assured of experiencing a positive encounter within a given day. The reason I am stating that a depressed individual is not certain of a positive encounter with another individual is because of the negative and moral decline of people in our society. Society is not emphasizing on the positive things in our world and culture.

Instead of focusing on positive solutions to help those afflicted with bipolar disorder and other mental illnesses, many are still contributing to the problem by focusing on the negative appearance of the mental condition rather than giving examples of depressed individuals who have successfully coped with the mental disease and are still mentally well and whole. It saddens me when the first thing considered when there is a murder, suicide, or mass shooting is whether or not the individual who committed those abominable crimes was suffering from mental illness, for example, bipolar disorder. Individuals with this severe mental condition should not be deemed by others as incorrigibly wicked.

This is what I mean when I say that some people in our society are still stereotyping and placing negative blame on those who may have a mental health struggle. Critical individuals in this nation and worldwide are definitely not focusing on the positive strides that individuals mentally affected by psychological illnesses and disorders have positively overcome throughout the years. Many who are still critical of those who are battling mental illnesses, such as bipolar disorder, are far from positive, and in my opinion, these individuals are negative, outdated, and small-minded.

Although the outside world can become negative toward those who face the daily grind of striving to sustain mental wellness and consistency, at the end of the day, the depressed individual is responsible for their positive mental imagery of themselves. When someone views themselves positively by focusing on many of their positive qualities and attributes, mental and physical confidence can arise within them. Experiencing manic and depressive episodes can definitely affect how positively the afflicted individual views life and others as well.

Within a day, so much can occur. I personally do not believe that an individual living 365 days, which equals a year, cannot at least consider something positive that happened to them. Though it is unrealistic for any individual to live all 365 days within a given year in a continuous mood of joy and happiness, one can still end each day on a positive note. Even a depressed person striving to experience consistency in mental comfort can still discover the positive highlights that the day has brought.

Positive activities can really help those enduring bipolar struggles. Although we potentially face negative events daily, we can all discover ways to do activities that bring out our creative sides. No individual will enjoy the same activities, and this is why every individual's activities are unique.

A depressed individual should identify at least one activity that brings out a tremendous amount of excitement in them. By nature, many bipolar people are creative beings. I am certain that an individual mentally affected by bipolar disorder will experience activities in life that they will eventually enjoy doing.

Of course, we, as a nation and society, have been economically impacted by the viral pandemic. Many individuals have been forced to discover alternative ways to produce income for themselves and their families. It is because of the intense pressure of trying to survive during these difficult and unprecedented times that many are not in a position to enjoy positive and creative activities.

Those who suffer from bipolar disorder must find time to experience some semblance of relaxation and fun. Their minds can, at times, become overloaded and fragile. When the individual coping with this psychological illness enjoys light and positive activities, they will have a chance of experiencing happiness and joy.

There must be a healthy mental balance for the depressed individual between leisure and the mandatory requirements of responsibility. Many people afflicted with bipolar disorder have children and families whom they are obligated to take care of. For an individual who suffers from this severe mental condition to live as productive and normal a life as possible, they must have something positive in life to do or anticipate.

As an individual who has lived with and coped with this mental disease for quite some time, I am always striving to focus on the positive things in life, not on the negative. In this world filled with hate and negativity, it is easy to focus on negative issues. The world and many of the people living in it are drifting further away from positive qualities and attributes that are influenced by love.

As a depressed individual, if you have support and love in your life, then continue to focus on that love to help you live successfully with this oftentimes challenging psychological disease. Some people who are afflicted with bipolar disorder do not have the luxury of having a loving and supportive family. Those who have love in their lives must rely on that love to maintain positive thoughts.

Life in this current world does not embody a positive standard of love and tolerance. Because of the world and society's lack of positive affection toward their members, some people with mental health disorders, such as bipolar disorder, do not feel any positive reinforcement from them. Thinking positively about oneself should be one's main focus.

Despite everything that occurs in this world, I believe that it is in need of a positive makeover. Individuals who are dealing with any type of mental disorder must understand how imperative it is to continue on a positive mental path. If a depressed individual can express their feelings to someone other than their psychiatrist/therapist, then that is something extremely positive.

Individuals who have battled bipolar disorder and been victorious over it must be heard. I believe that now, although there will always be a stigma attached to having a mental illness, more bearers are now coming forward to talk about their mental health struggles. Experiencing the peaks and valleys of bipolar disorder can make the bearer of the condition question if there is a way to have a positive perspective when it comes to dealing with it.

Illnesses and sicknesses are a part of life. There are reasons beyond my finite comprehension why some are destined to experience mental health illnesses. Today, in the current climate that we are living in, the one positive takeaway that I can gather from becoming afflicted with mental illnesses, such as bipolar disorder, is that there are people ready and willing to listen to all whose minds are filled with chaos and whose thoughts and feelings are filled with either anxiety or hopelessness.

Having twenty-four-hour hotlines for those who do not feel supported and have no one to relate to because of their mental challenges is something that I consider positive for the depressed person. Mental health crisis experts should be commended for their listening ears and positive feedback. Depressed individuals will respond positively when someone other than a doctor, loved one, close friend, or associate is focused on their mental health concerns and needs.

Each day that we live, the positive state of the world and society is increasingly diminishing. I will not state that it is easy to live one's life, trying to focus on the positive aspects of it. As we have all seen in recent years, calamity and destruction can strike at any moment despite having a positive attitude and mindset.

One must strive to find a positive perspective in life despite all the challenges and crises they may encounter mentally. The best part of living for the positive things in life is that they are always within our grasp. No matter how difficult life may become, an individual can still learn something positive from that experience or adversity.

I have learned something positive about myself after battling bipolar disorder for so long. The positive attribute that I discovered about myself is that I can be resilient and courageous. When I focused on the positive qualities that I found in myself, I commenced to reflect upon the struggles I experienced and ultimately overcame them despite my bipolar disorder. At the core of each individual affected by this severe mental disease is a positive perception that lies deep within.

Situations and circumstances dictate whether one will have a positive attitude and mindset. Someone who suffers from bipolar disorder should not allow this mental health condition to have a negative effect on their life. If a depressed individual is not careful, this mental disorder will cause them to wallow in pity and pessimism.

When a doctor/therapist says that there is no cure for bipolar disorder, focusing on positive things in life becomes difficult. Individuals with mental disorders must not replay the doctor's prognosis repetitively in their minds. Replaying what could be considered grim with regard to their mental health can essentially make them lose hope and optimism for their future.

Some may suggest that someone who has this mental condition should not have a positive outlook. One who is not affected by bipolar disorder may not understand how a depressed individual remains positive despite the illness's long-lasting impact on their life. Those who can somehow live successfully with bipolar disorder have victory over the lifelong psychological disease because they have learned how to focus on positive things.

For those having a difficult time trying to sustain a positive mindset, I would suggest that you do not succumb to all the negativity going on in the world and, in many cases, in your environment. As an individual who personally understands how difficult it can become to maintain a positive mental attitude consistently, I am living proof that a depressed individual can be optimistic. The key to continuous success with this mental condition is the development of a positive attitude in life.

Having a positive attitude and perspective on life is rare when you factor in the negative state of the world and society. It is also uncommon for those with bipolar disorder to live their lives with a positive mentality. This psychological disorder generally does not equate to the affected individual having consistency in their mood.

Individuals who are afflicted with bipolar disorder are, in many instances, considered "moody." There are some whose moods are so inconsistent that those in close contact or proximity to them never know what their mood will be. With the right dosage of medicine and mental therapy, the chances for those who suffer from mental conditions to focus on the positive things in their lives while sustaining a positive mood become significantly greater.

An individual who can focus on what is positive in their life will develop contentment and maturity. I believe that a bipolar individual is also capable of becoming optimistic and content. Remember, every individual, including those who are in the midst of a mental health battle, can discover all of the positive things that they are blessed with, which include the opportunity to make tomorrow better than yesterday.

Setting realistic goals and accomplishing them will help anyone discover what is positive in their life. I am aware that there are varying levels of goals. It is always wise to use goals in life as positive "stepping stones" for greater ones.

I was able to do just that in my life. Although I went through a plethora of difficulties as a result of having bipolar disorder, today I cannot help but be optimistic, especially when I consider how dire my experiences and episodes with the psychological illness were. If you, as a depressed individual, can view the fact that you are still living as something positive in your life, then you can determine for yourself that seeing another day is definitely something that must be viewed as a positive accomplishment.

Though bipolar disorder is treatable and controllable today, it also has an aspect that may not allow the affected individual to become optimistic. Some people who have the psychological disease do not foresee anything in their lives that can be deemed positive. Individuals with that mindset and attitude will automatically shut down mentally.

As I previously stated, bipolar disorder affects not just thousands of people in this nation but millions in this country and worldwide. Out of the millions who are significantly affected by this psychological disease, I wonder what percentage of those mentally affected can discover and determine what and who in their life is a positive influence. In my opinion, depressed individuals must realize something positive in their life with whom they feel confident and can rely on.

Some people are so deep within the darkness of this mental condition that they do not stop and consider all of the positive components that contribute to their life. Those who cannot determine anything positive in their lives will sink deeper into the abyss of this severe mental disorder. In this life, there are a plethora of negative occurrences because such is life.

Life is not meant for any individual to live without experiencing both the positive and negative extremes of it. It is extremely foolish to think that every day will always be filled with "rainbows and sunshine." On the other hand, life does not have to be dark and unpleasant either.

I will not be oblivious to all the negative and tragic events that seem to be constantly and increasingly occurring. One might suggest that there is no need to discover any positive aspects of life because the world and its people are headed for trouble and destruction. As a mere human and also a fellow depressed person, I am cognizant of the fact that, with the decline of our society, there is little hope that this turbulent society as a whole can offer.

Though society does not offer optimism, this does not mean that one cannot delve this quality within oneself. This is the very reason one should always look toward the Creator. When a depressed individual can make a genuine connection with Him, then they will soon realize how the positive things in their life were there all along.

Once an individual living with bipolar disorder becomes optimistic, a successful life is on the horizon. It is not easy to remain optimistic in the midst of a mental health struggle. Life itself is a battle and definitely, at times, a detriment to an individual's overall health.

Bipolar disorder and optimism usually do not go hand in hand. This is a mental illness that typically results in deep sorrow and sadness for the bearer as well as for those in the bearer's life. When you factor in all of the chaos and destruction in the world and society, positive optimism is a rarity.

I wholeheartedly believe that some who are resistant to medication management and therapy, disregarding it as vital, are essentially affecting their own potential for perceiving life in a positive manner. Personally, I disagree with those who do not view therapy and medication management as something positive. Though there is no cure for bipolar disorder, depressed individuals has the opportunity to experience optimism when they become receptive to the process of lifelong treatment and therapy.

Many people opposed to receiving treatment for this mental health condition do not understand how it is one of the key contributing factors to their perception of the things in life that they can deem positive. A doctor/therapist can help a depressed individual realize how positive it is to have prolonged mental wellness. The more a sufferer of bipolar disorder resists treatment and advice from a competent doctor, the less likely it is that they can develop a positive viewpoint.

Now I am not in any way stating that once an individual with a mental disorder finally yields to therapy, they will suddenly focus on what is positive in their life, but I believe that counseling for a significant amount of time can help them come to that conclusion. Journeying through life while focusing on its positive aspects is crucial for bipolar individuals. If individuals with psychological conditions can somehow have positive thoughts, then their minds and mood will also have that same mindset.

Before one can focus on what in their life is positive, they may have to learn how to self-examine and assess. We all must do this to develop a positive attitude. No depressed individual should remain in a negative and depressive state of mind, although this mental disorder is present.

Optimism always yields to hope, and hope is something that every individual must have in these times of struggle. Those who have hope in life are more likely to experience happiness despite the outside forces in this world. Individuals who are coping with bipolar disorder do not have to allow external factors to influence them to continuously focus on the negative and harmful things in life.

How do you get to the point of focusing on what is positive in your life? Firstly, take an inventory of their life. Secondly, if you cannot discover the current positive things in life, then try to reflect upon memories. Thirdly, if the inventory of your life is not yielding optimism and you do not have previous positive memories, then strive to create new and present ones.

Our minds are generally controlled by what we ultimately think. Despite all the negativity occurring in the world today, optimistic thoughts are what will basically get one through the difficulties and adversities in life. In a depressed individual's life, it is never easy to experience thoughts of hope and optimism when mentally affected by bipolar disorder.

Many who are in the midst of a psychotic episode are not focused on what is positive in their lives during that specific time. Individuals who suffer from this severe mental condition would like nothing more than to have a positive perception of life, but in some extreme cases, their minds will not allow them to. Hopefully, one who is a bearer of this life-changing mental disease will eventually develop a positive perspective and outlook on life.

Some people who battle bipolar disorder cannot come to terms with having an optimistic point of view. As one who has overcome and coped successfully with this mental condition, I am saddened by that fact. Personally, while coping with this disorder, I have experienced many times when I could not determine anything positive that I considered worthy of living through in my life.

This is a perilous mentality to have in the life of a bipolar sufferer. When they cannot or will not identify the things and people in their lives who give them hope or optimism, they can ultimately succumb emotionally and physically to this psychological condition. It is up to them to decide if their focus will be on either the optimistic things in this life or the pessimistic things that can inflict more harm than good in their minds.

The world in which we live has enough negativity to last throughout all of eternity. Those who are coping with and battling bipolar disorder should not surrender to the negative stigma attached to this severe mental illness. Instead, the depressed person needs to focus and be committed to every positive encounter and interaction that they have experienced or have previously experienced.

A depressed individual must always focus on positive situations and circumstances to sustain mental wellness. An individual who is bipolar will not experience prolonged success with this psychological disorder while focusing on negative things in life. Consistency in mental stability is evident in a depressed person's life when their primary focus is on all of the positive things that they can potentially experience.

Chapter 6

Strive for a Consistent Mood

Mood consistency is the primary goal for the bipolar individual. Bipolar disorder can negatively affect the bearer's mood. There are some whose mood is significantly unbalanced.

It is highly uncommon for any individual to remain in a consistent mood every day of the year. Individuals who are not bipolar do not always have a positive temperament. If those who do not suffer from this mental disorder sometimes struggle with having a consistent mood, then the depressed person might be in a long-lasting and never-ending mood battle.

The prevailing stereotype for many who are mentally affected by bipolar disorder is that the depressed individual is "moody." Some naively think that all individuals who struggle with this mental condition are incapable of experiencing a consistent mood. I believe that with the right medicine and the development of tools to cope with life's stressors and triggers, depressed individuals have a chance to live their life with a consistent temperament.

Many who are in the midst of a bipolar struggle may not be aware of the inconsistency in their mood. Loved ones and close friends who frequently interact with the depressed individual would notice if the individual is "moody." When it comes to the mood of bipolar individuals, the chemical balance in their brains can be a key factor in their mood changes.

Medication and therapy can significantly help the mentally affected individual to become more balanced in their mood. Some individuals who experience the extreme depressive lows of the mental disorder cannot help the way that they feel. If every day is filled with darkness, then their mood will also become sullen and dark.

A consistent mood is only accomplished when the affected individual, who is the bearer of the mental condition, learns how to cope with it. Bipolar disorder is unpredictable. With regard to a depressed individual's mood, it can also result in uncertainty.

This is one reason bipolar disorder is a mood disorder, which is highly considered a psychological condition that is difficult to pinpoint and predict. Psychiatrists are always concerned about the mood of an individual afflicted with the mental disease. Most mental health professionals will ask about their patient's temperaments in the midst of a therapy session.

What constitutes a consistent mood? From my perspective, as an individual who has experienced this mood and mental disorder for several years, I have been able to successfully have a positive and consistent mood when I did what was required of me. For instance, I take the medicine prescribed by my doctor consistently without deviating from it. Also, I try to become personally aware of my own behavior and conduct. Lastly, I avoid emotional triggers that could negatively affect my mood and emotional state.

Sufferers of bipolar disorder are not typically known to have a consistent mood. Though I am diagnosed with the mental disorder, I would like to defy the perception from others that every bipolar individual suffers from moodiness.

One of the biggest compliments I have received since being diagnosed with bipolar disorder is that I have always remained the same. My uncle gave me that compliment many years ago. After being commended for my consistent mood, I have strived to maintain that pattern ever since.

Some struggle with their mood toward others. Just like the unpredictability of the constantly changing weather, some with mental conditions may be nice in one instant, then in another instant, they become mean and surly. Because of my experiences with other individuals with the same mental disorder, I know what it is like to encounter a depressed person who has an unbalanced mood and temperament.

If someone you know and love is mentally affected by bipolar disorder and has moody behavior toward you, try not to take it personally. As I previously stated, the mood of the depressed individual may not have anything to do with their personality. The behavior can be derived from the effects of the illness itself.

Finding the right mood balance is critical to living with and coping with this severe psychological condition. I can only imagine the challenge that many psychiatrists and mental health professionals face when dealing with individuals with extreme cases of bipolar disorder. It is difficult to treat individuals whose conduct and behavior are uncooperative.

There is always a glimmer of hope for those struggling to remain consistent in their mood and significantly improve in that area. Of course, when it comes to any kind of improvement, patience must be considered. Years of medication management and intense therapy are imperative in the process of sustaining a relatively balanced mood level.

In my own battle with bipolar disorder, I was fortunate enough to understand how maintaining a positive and consistent mood would become a key to having any semblance of success in coping and living successfully with this lifelong battle with this mental illness. If one's mood is balanced and sustained, then there is a greater chance for the depressed individual to live a life of relative normalcy. A life of normalcy for them is when they are not restricted by their mood to perform various activities the same as those who are not mentally ill.

In other words, an individual who is affected by this severe mental condition does not have to allow their mood to enslave them. Mental freedom becomes a likely reality when the individual's mood level is well-balanced and in sync. Continuous mental wellness typically means that the mentally affected individual has their mood in order.

Doing positive activities that you enjoy regularly can lead to a mentally consistent mood. For instance, I look forward to exercising each day. This is an activity that has resulted in a consistent mood for years.

Now I am cognizant of the fact that some people do not like to partake in daily exercise. Although exercising is not for everyone, I am sure that there are other activities that one could partake in that can influence one to have a consistent mood. In the daytime, the sun is usually out, and studies have proven in previous years that some form of sun exposure can help with an individual's overall mood.

If spending time outdoors is not your cup of tea, then discovering indoor activities within the friendly confines of your home could also be beneficial to your temperament. The key to having a positive and consistent mood is doing things that will bring joy and happiness into one's life. Also, an individual with bipolar disorder must not do an activity just for the sake of doing it.

When someone does something they do not love and enjoy, of course, it will have a negative effect on their temperament. I stated earlier how exercising continuously will significantly improve an individual's mood. But realistically, some will not take heed to the overall benefits of this particular activity.

Somehow, those who are mentally affected by bipolar disorder must find various ways to develop a consistent temperament. I know that sleeping all day will not dramatically improve a depressed individual's mood. One has to do something throughout the day for a substantial amount of time to experience a mood of consistency.

With all of the utter chaos in the midst of this world and society, it is more apparent than ever before that during these uncertain times, an individual must learn how to strive for a long-lasting mental balance. There is so much tragic heartbreak occurring each day that having a consistent mood is a rare occurrence. Temperament and moods do not always have to be influenced by society or one's environment.

Moods are influenced by what an individual feels internally. With regard to a depressed person, he or she has to realize and understand that consistency in their mood is only experienced when the individual is able to recognize their own behavior. Advancing in the development of one's own mental conduct is vital to the individual who is affected by bipolar disorder.

Individuals who enjoy consistency in their mood cannot experience it without someone who is there to help them. Supportive loved ones and friends who are transparent and honest but not overbearing in their approach to the bearer of the psychological condition can always tell the depressed individual when their mood is unstable. Once the affected individual's support system pinpoints the individual's mood of instability, then it is up to them to take heed and listen.

Striving and anticipating a better tomorrow is what many who are battling this psychological disease must do to experience a consistent temperament. From a spiritual perspective, the world in which we live does not edify our minds. There is something greater than this current world that far outweighs what an individual might think or feel.

If a depressed individual can adopt that attitude and mindset, then the chances of them having a consistent mood are greater than before their bipolar disorder diagnosis. Every individual who has ever become afflicted with this severe mental illness would love nothing more than to have a consistent mood. Some people who have the mental disorder ignorantly think that if they self-medicate with alcohol and other substances, their mood will dramatically improve and be consistent.

In fact, chemical substances and other recreational drugs will never help a depressed individual's chances of experiencing mental and mood consistency. Many of those who abuse these substances are not anticipating a better tomorrow. These particular individuals are only living for the moment.

When it comes to having consistency in one's mood, it does not mean that the individual will never experience moments of sadness and grief. Of course, when a loved one or close friend passes away, a depressed individual will not be able to have a joyful mood. It is during those times of grief that one should not expect a mentally affected person to immediately become consistent mentally.

The difference between a depressed individual having a bout of grief and sadness and a mentally affected individual whose mood is always filled with continuous sadness is that the individual with a consistent mood does not have prolonged depression and sorrow. After the individual with the consistent temperament has grieved because of a loss, they will return to their temperament. We all have or will one day experience losing someone close to us.

It is normal to have feelings of sorrow, but for a depressed person, the loss of someone close to them can become a trigger and ultimately have a negative effect on their mood. An individual who is mentally affected by bipolar disorder must be carefully monitored when a loss of life is experienced. I am cognizant of the fact that discussing the loss of life is not a popular topic of discussion for anyone.

In the world of today, death is a grim reality. Individuals who live with and cope with bipolar disorder each day do not have to live in continual mental agony. Instead, they should strive to live, hoping for another tomorrow.

Anticipation for the individual who is the bearer of this mental condition is hugely important. One who can look forward in life is an individual whose mood is typically positive. Although life is not always filled with overwhelming joy, an individual's mood does not have to be influenced by it.

Perseverance and persistency are qualities that we would all love to have. If bipolar individuals desire to have a consistent mood, then these specific qualities are an option. It requires an enormous amount of persistence in a depressed individual's quest to acquire a consistent mood level.

When negative events occur in an individual affected by bipolar disorder, it can have a devastating effect on them. As a depressed individual myself, I try not to succumb to events in life that are tragically occurring at an alarming rate. No one can do anything about what will inevitably occur, but we all can react and respond with our mood, becoming either negative or positive.

Our moods are extremely vital to how well or poorly we will respond to any given situation or circumstance. I am mindful of the fact that when faced with a life-altering circumstance, an individual might not be in the greatest of moods. Who could blame them when they have to uproot their lives because of circumstances beyond their control? Some sufferers of bipolar disorder do not have a positive and consistent mood when situations and circumstances are positive and favorable.

I believe that individuals who are mentally affected by bipolar disorder can experience days, months, and even years of mental wellness and wholeness when they can somehow get their mood levels controlled. This is why the right type of medication and treatment for the depressed individual is extremely significant. Individuals who are bipolar must not continue in frustration if initially, their mood is not consistent.

The development of mood consistency is, in many cases, long and gradual. In some instances, an individual will give up on having a consistent mood when they feel as though the medication is not working properly. Many who experience this scenario naively conclude that their mood will always be the way it is, which can be negative and unstable.

My mood was unstable and inconsistent for several years before it reached a level of consistency. Now I am thankful that it has remained that way for over ten years. When it comes to having a consistent mood level, every depressed individual and their family must remain hopeful and optimistic that one day they can also experience the joy of having a stabilized mood.

Sadly, every individual who is living with and coping with bipolar disorder will not always be successful in maintaining a consistent mood. Unfortunately, this is just the harsh reality. Some have an excessive amount of issues with regard to their mood that can potentially threaten their optimism for a mood change.

I cannot discuss the potential of an individual with this mental disorder becoming stable in their mood without stating the fact that not all will experience long-term mood stability. Please do not mistake me for being a Debbie Downer or a pessimist. Realistically, if a third of individuals who are mentally affected by this psychological disease can experience mood stability, then that should be considered a success in the bipolar community.

Awareness of what could trigger a mood of sadness and despair is crucial for the sufferer of this psychological disorder. Thoughts of sorrow will essentially equate to a negative mood. Some of those who are coping with and living with bipolar disorder are prisoners of their own temperament. Those who are slaves to their own moodiness do not envision any other way to live their lives. Life is never joyous when your mood is not consistent and stable. It is a life that is filled with deep despair and turmoil.

In this day and age, it does not require much for any individual, including those who are bearers of bipolar disorder, to experience unstable moods. A depressed individual is in the minority when he or she can develop a consistent mood. Each bipolar sufferer should strive to be among this rare group.

A consistent and stable mood for the depressed individual is viewed as a commodity. In other words, because consistency in one's overall mood can become a rarity, I am certain that it is highly valued by those who suffer from bipolar disorder. Because of the unpredictability of this psychological disease, a depressed person cannot be assured of having a consistent mood.

The acquisition of a mood balance can elude those who are not doing their part to remain mentally stable. Though a psychiatrist/therapist monitors a depressed individual, the individual must also monitor their own temperament. An effective way to monitor one's mood and behavior is by keeping a diary or a daily journal.

A licensed and board-certified psychiatrist or mental health expert can effectively learn how to treat the mood disorder when they can assess what the depressed individual might have written. I am mindful that, in some cases, doctors and psychiatrists might tend to avoid relying heavily on a mentally affected person's diary or journal entries to honor privacy of that particular individual.

Bipolar disorder, when the depressed individual is in a depressive state, a mood of sadness is difficult for bipolar individuals to break away from. In this particular mental state, it seems that the individual's mind is raining with thoughts of hopelessness. An individual who experiences long bouts of sadness and darkness is essentially headed in a precarious direction in life.

Hopefully, a depressed individual experiencing those depressive moods can somehow overcome them. No individual in a depressive mood can miraculously shake out of it. Individuals who tell those who are in the midst of a depressive episode to "snap out of it are oblivious and insensitive to the depressed individual's mood and feelings.

Bipolar bearers must identify the things that can trigger their mood of uncontrollable sadness. Once those mood triggers are accurately pinpointed, the individual should do everything in their power not to dwell on them. Remaining in a mood of stability is possible when the bearer of this psychological disease understands and learns how to cope with mental stressors.

Winning the battle over bipolar disorder requires that the affected individual acquire a consistent mood. There is no other way that a depressed person can successfully overcome it. A consistent mood must become their number one goal.

When a depressed individual experiences a mood of consistency, they will become more engaging and confident. Think about it. Once they regain confidence because of a consistent mood, they can accomplish all sorts of dreams and goals in life.

In my life, some are not aware that I have bipolar disorder. Because I strive to become the same person each time when interacting, my mood is not much of an issue. I must admit that my consistent mood did not occur immediately.

For many years, medication management, counseling, and self-examination have been critical components of maintaining a consistent mood. The depressed individual must become willing to do those things to maintain a sustainable mood. Many of those who suffer from bipolar disorder are doing themselves a disservice by not following the instructions and guidelines for maintaining mood stability.

One can have a stable mood when the individual does not rebel against the doctor's suggestions. Some find themselves in predicaments when they trust their own plans to combat this mental condition. As an individual who has acted in rebellion as far as not considering how imperative it is to take the prescribed psychotropic medicine, I had to realize that this medicine does help with consistency in my thoughts, especially when it comes to my mood.

Stress can affect any individual's outlook and mood. Every individual who experiences this mental disorder will not react the same way to issues and problems in life. It really does matter how a depressed individual responds to adversities because if the individual's mood is negatively affected by life's mishaps, then their overall temperament might suffer.

An individual's success in anything in life is derived from persistence and determination. A depressed person must have those attributes to maintain a healthy and balanced mood for a vast amount of time. Mood stability is essential to the individual who is coping with and living with bipolar disorder.

No mentally ill individual can be victorious over this psychological disease without fully investing in getting their mood in check. Commitment to the mental process of mood consistency can be difficult, but it is not impossible to achieve. One who is in the midst of a depressive episode can acquire hope and optimism that their depressive mood and state of mind will eventually subside. With the right medicine, commitment to mood and wellness, and a reliable support system, their moodiness will not have any lingering effects.

Patience, persistence, and perseverance are needed for the individual experiencing mental anguish from this psychological illness to finally enjoy mood stability. If you or someone you love is having a difficult time with mood consistency, try not to lose hope for them. Personally, I have seen how my mood has drastically improved.

I can recall my mood and state of mind when I was in the midst of a horrific depressive episode. During that time, I had been in a depressive mood for approximately a year. The year was 1996, and although I did not contemplate suicide, my mood was not at all in the positive state it is today.

Sure, I did fun activities, which many would consider enjoyable, but I can recall how, during almost that entire year, I commenced to struggle with my mood level. My psychiatrist at that time almost gave up on me because the depressive mood I had was not improving. Whether the news that I received was optimistic, it did not influence my temperament in any way.

As I reflect on my mood at that time of difficulty, it is amazing how I have been able to now have a successful mood level and balance. The mood that I had back then compared to today is a total transformation from what it was decades ago. You might be asking yourself, *What changed in his life for him to experience a positive mood change?* I believe that it was not necessarily the medication that aided a positive transformation in my mood.

I had triggers in my life that had a negative effect on me. For example, the company I associated with negatively influenced my temperament. Also, the lifestyle that I practiced negatively affected my mood.

When that particular year was finally over, I desired to usher in the New Year with a new mood and perspective. Did it take time to acquire a positive mood and mental stability? Of course, it did. I would not be able to experience a positive and consistent mood without exercising patience and perseverance.

The mood of a bipolar individual can have two extremes. Either they are experiencing an unrealistic mood of great euphoria in the manic phase or the depths of extreme gloominess and sadness, which will equate to a mood of despair. A balanced mood is acquired when the depressed individual's mood is not too high or too low but is right in the middle of the mood spectrum.

Although the process of mental consistency can be extremely challenging, consistency in one's mood does not have to become burdensome. One must always have enough patience and hope to understand that their mood and temperament need time to evolve. Striving for mood consistency in a world and society filled with triggers and stress may seem unattainable, but with the correct treatment and persistence, an individual dealing with mood inconsistency can ultimately achieve their mood balance.

Beginning each day in a consistent mood, though difficult, can be experienced by an individual who just happens to be bipolar. If the depressed person has any chance of successfully coping with bipolar disorder, their mood must be stabilized and balanced. Now the depressed individual's mood should not become fully monotonous or unresponsive in living their life but consistent and positive when properly treated.

No one desires to be around someone who is consistently moody each day. The individual who is struggling with bipolar illness may not be the most pleasant person to be around. Individuals who are in the midst of an episode can be oblivious to how they are acting and behaving toward others.

It requires a special individual in the life of the person experiencing anger and irritability as a result of this psychological disease to continue to remain in their life despite the depressed person's "moody behavior." Remember, bipolar disorder is a chemical imbalance in the brain. If your brain is not functioning properly, it can have a negative effect on your mood and emotions.

A depressed individual who may be considered "moody" by those closest to them also deserves to be respected and loved. Though dealing with someone unpredictable in their behavior is not easy, their family and friends should always remain hopeful and optimistic that either the depressed individual's behavior will change for the better or that they will return to the person they were before the onset of this mental condition. I am not oblivious to the fact that the mood of some who are battling this mental disease may not improve or develop consistency to successfully overcome the negative aspects of bipolar disorder.

This psychological illness can weigh heavily on the mood and emotions of the mentally affected individual. An individual experiencing irritability and mood inconsistency will not always be able to control their emotions and feelings. It is due to that fact that love and patience should be required and given.

One must view the "moodiness" of an individual who is coping and dealing with bipolar disorder as one of the various symptoms of their psychological condition. When those who are in the company of an individual who is always irritated can realize that the illness itself influences the affected person's behavior, then those closest to the individual will not be as offended as they were by the depressed individual's mood and behavior before the diagnosis. As a fellow bearer of this psychological disease, I know that it can be difficult to maintain a consistent and stable mood for an enormous amount of time.

Somehow and someway, the individual affected by bipolar disorder should become convinced that their condition and mood will gradually stabilize. The mood of a stabilized individual is typically positive and pleasant. To experience a positive mood balance, the depressed person must not have a closed mind when it comes to complying with what must be done in the treatment process.

Team effort is vital in combating mood inconsistency. The depressed individual, the doctor/therapist, and the individual's support system must all work hand in hand. The mentally affected person has to trust that the doctor can help with the stabilization of their mood.

Once the depressed individual welcomes all that encompasses a consistent mood, then I am certain that there will not be as many days of "moodiness." Those who are in the bipolar battle should be receptive to discovering ways of maintaining mood consistency. Learning more about their condition, along with what can trigger a negative mood, can drastically help them tremendously with the mental illness.

It is imperative for the depressed person to write down how they are feeling each day. When one reads on paper their own thoughts and feelings, they can discover their mood. Bipolar disorder does not have to be victorious in the affected individual's level of mood consistency. I personally believe that they can live each day with a positive temperament. Although life itself is never perfect, their moods will also not be flawless. There is so much within a given day that we all experience that can have an impact on our mood and emotions.

Depressed individuals must always be cognizant of their feelings and how a situation or circumstance will affect them positively or negatively. The main goal for all who are mentally affected by bipolar disorder is to continue to experience a healthy mood level and balance. Bipolar individuals cannot reach a balanced mood level without being properly medicated.

Unfortunately, there is no other way. When an individual is initially diagnosed with bipolar disorder, their mood levels are typically out of sorts. It is due to the unbalanced mood levels that the depressed individual must take psychotropic medicine to help their levels improve.

They may not be mindful of how they are contributing to their own unbalanced mood level when they rebel and refuse to take the medicine prescribed by a licensed and board-certified psychiatrist. This is also why most psychiatrists do periodic bloodwork from time to time. Taking the prescribed medicine will definitely help the depressed individual feel drastically better and have balanced mood levels.

Consistency in a bipolar sufferer's mood is vital because, in many cases, it helps them experience some semblance of normalcy in life. An individual who is currently struggling to maintain a consistent mood must realize within themselves that they are highly unqualified to be mood stabilizers. Each mentally affected individual should not make the mistake of minimizing the importance of mood stability. If bipolar individuals ultimately recognizes the significance of mood consistency and a stabilized and balanced mood, then they are on the road to mental redemption.

Chapter 7

Think Wellness, Not Sickness

Sickness and disease have been present in this world and society for many centuries. Sometimes, we, as a culture and society, are numb to the effects of illnesses. One who suffers from bipolar disorder should not allow the mental disorder to affect how they view themselves.

For instance, some may think that bipolar individuals must never think that they have any chance of mental wellness. My suggestion to them is to strive to prove those who have a negative stereotype wrong. An individual who happens to have bipolar disorder must develop thoughts of mental wellness and wholeness instead of sickness.

When someone is constantly reiterating to you that you are bipolar or mentally ill, and after hearing others state that to you day after day, it can be embedded in your mind. It does not offer any hope to the depressed individual when they are continuously reminded of their condition. So hearing that one is mentally ill consistently will result in the mentally affected individual acting out or having a defeatist mindset.

In the news each day, there is usually some reference to an individual who is mentally ill. Many who are psychologically affected by this mental disease do not have any hope of improvement. I am cognizant of the fact that many of us are products of our self-perception and image.

If one thinks that they are mentally well, then there is a possibility that the mind, thoughts, and other parts of their body can be positively affected. The mind is an important factor in determining whether or not an individual deems themselves well or not. Every depressed individual can think about mental wellness.

We are all in control of our minds and thoughts. Sure, some can tell us how or what to think, but one's mind belongs to oneself and not any other individual. Personally, I have been reminded in the past about the mental condition that I have.

There were times that I must admit that I was not too confident that I would ever be mentally well. For years, I struggled with thoughts of sickness. It is due to those negative thoughts that I commenced to think of myself as an individual who suffers from a mental illness.

One day, my thoughts about illness and sickness changed. I decided mentally that I would try to change my negative thought pattern. First, I commence to read and watch programs by which I can be mentally inspired. I love drawing inspiration from individuals who, as others have said, cannot achieve what they set out to do, although these particular individuals encountered tremendous adversity.

Others might have told the overachiever that there was no way they would ever accomplish what they desired to do. Instead, the individual who faced adversity and resistance from others listened to their own mind and achieved what others said they could not. The mentally affected individual could also gain a mental edge over the psychological disease through the wellness of thoughts.

My thoughts on mental wellness have been instrumental in becoming victorious over this severe mental disorder. Today, I do not think of myself as an individual who happens to have a mental condition. Now I simply refer to myself as a capable human being who has experienced adversities with regard to mental illness and as an individual who refers to himself as mentally whole and fit.

I believe that thoughts are extremely vital to the success of a depressed individual in remaining on the right mental course. People can tell anyone anything with regard to one's health, but when it comes to someone with a mental condition, such as bipolar disorder, it is ultimately the affected individual's thoughts that influence them to continue to sustain thoughts about wellness. How does an individual overcome health conditions like breast cancer or heart disease? In my opinion, an individual who has those particular health issues will not overcome them without first having the right mental outlook or mentality.

Yes, I do believe that doctors and medicine can and will help any individual with significant health conditions improve. But I also believe that how an individual perceives their chances of improvement plays a crucial role. Some individuals are given only hours or even months to live, and somehow, some of these same individuals have defied the odds and lived beyond the specified time that the doctor said would be their demise.

So if it were not the treatment or the doctor that was a contributing factor in someone outliving their prognosis, then one who is on the outside looking in can only come to a couple of conclusions. The first conclusion is that the individual affected had a plethora of support. Another conclusion is the individual's thoughts and will.

Though bipolar disorder is a mood and mental concern for millions, it is also a health concern that some do not view in the same way as other health conditions. Who is to say that an individual with and living with this mental disease cannot also surprise and defy the doctor's or psychiatrist's long-term prognosis? Millions in this country and around the world have just as much of a chance of improving from a severe health condition as others who may have been in a far worse health predicament. When it comes to victory over bipolar disorder, the thoughts of the depressed individual can result in good overall mental health.

Some in our world and society do not emphasize prolonged mental wellness and success over this mental illness. Most are discussing the illness' effect instead of how some have managed to combat the psychological illness by remaining mentally well. Individuals who bear this psychological condition also can cope successfully with the condition through positive thoughts of mental wellness, which the mind influences.

We, as human beings, tend to harp on our limitations. Some people believe that they cannot do or achieve a certain goal in life because of their insecurity or inadequacy. Individuals who are living with bipolar disorder must not limit themselves with regard to mental wellness by thinking that they will always be afflicted by this mental condition.

One who has dealt with various manic and depressive episodes should never feel as though these mental experiences are forever. Medication and therapy can help the mental episodes subside. Though the process of recovering from manic and depressive episodes is difficult in most cases, there is always a chance that the depressed individual can enjoy mental wholeness rather than sickness.

No individual should live their life constantly thinking about their particular health challenge. Those who are coping with bipolar disorder do not have to face each day with their illness constantly on their mind. Health and wellness will always elude the individual whose mind is bombarded with continuous thoughts about their mental health.

Though personally, I have experienced both manic and depressive episodes in the past, these episodes are not constantly in my thoughts. I can recall just about every episode that I have ever experienced. It will do more harm than good to reflect on those times when I was struggling mentally.

For individuals who are coping with and dealing with bipolar disorder, I am in no way suggesting that they suppress those times when the illness had dominion. What I am recommending to the depressed individual is that they not remain in the same mental state and mindset.

Mentally affected individuals who have thrived in life are not influenced by their past behaviors. Thriving in life does not mean that the individual is experiencing an enormous amount of monetary success. Real success for individuals living with bipolar disorder is when they can experience consistency in mental wellness.

The one thing that individuals affected by this psychological disorder should never do is place limitations on their mental improvement. Bipolar disorder does not have to keep the affected individual in the same state of agony and anguish. This is why those who have lived with the mental condition for a substantial amount of time must always envision victory over it.

Hope and optimism are key factors in one's thoughts about mental wellness and wholeness. Doctors and therapists do play a vital role in the mental health of a depressed individual, but ultimately, the thoughts of the individual, whether positive or negative, will essentially prevail. The difference between a depressed individual enjoying continuous mental wellness and an individual who is not is basically predicated on their internal outlook and perception of life and mental health.

Stability and consistency in one's thoughts will not lead to sickness for the individual living with this particular mental disorder. Before a depressed person can begin to experience wellness, the condition itself has to be controlled. Thoughts that can lead to either a manic or depressive episode must be dealt with aggressively and immediately.

A depressed individual must not become timid or passive in their approach to mental stability and wellness. In other words, the mentally affected individual has to consciously decide if they will continue to allow their thoughts to mentally defeat them or become active in developing positive thoughts. Our thoughts are extremely important, especially for those who are battling any type of mental illness.

I have been able to maintain mental wellness for over a decade because of my thoughts of good health, not just mentally but throughout my entire body. Mental wellness has everything to do with how one thinks and feels. No one can fake their way into sustainability with regard to their mental health.

Some might suggest that one "fakes it until one makes it." How can anyone maintain a facade of mental wellness? I believe that this mindset causes damage to a depressed individual's psyche. For instance, when someone pretends to be something that they are not, they are not being truthful to themselves.

One has to wholeheartedly believe in their mind and heart that they have improved from this severe mental disorder. If one internally believes that improvement has been made mentally, then others will also take heed. There is nothing that I like better than to see the mental wellness of a depressed individual stand the test of time.

The culmination of one's thoughts determines how well an individual actually is. When it comes to someone who is bipolar, typically, the individual's thoughts will reflect their behavior and/or conduct. Depressed individuals who are ill or experiencing a psychotic episode may not be aware of how their thoughts are, in many cases, one of the culprits with regard to the individual not being well mentally.

We all have to think to make it through a given day. Thinking, essentially, leads to decisions. Those who are not mentally well typically make the wrong ones.

Although we as humans are always prone to committing mistakes, most people who are mentally well will commit errors in life, but they will make more sound decisions. This is one way of knowing if an individual is thinking well mentally. Many who are mentally ill with bipolar disorder may make decisions while in the midst of a manic or depressive episode that, when they are in their right frame of mind or mental state, they would never entertain.

Living constantly in a state of regret will negatively affect how an individual acts and feels toward oneself and others. Mental wellness and regret are never synonymous. If one is to have positive thoughts of mental consistency, then that individual must not allow regret from a past situation or being diagnosed with a mental illness to have precedence.

Sickly thoughts will affect the mind of the individual who is experiencing extreme symptoms of bipolar illness. It is difficult to have thoughts of mental wellness when the mental health environment of the bipolar individual is not positive. We are living in a time in which an individual's mental health is continuously challenged.

Thoughts of mental wellness and wholeness are needed if the mentally affected individual plans to overcome and live successfully with this severe mental disorder. I believe that genuine confidence will help them think of mental wellness instead of sickness and defeat. A depressed individual owes it to himself or herself to become mentally stable and whole.

For a mentally affected individual to continue to think of mental wellness, they must first believe and have faith within their mind that they can be stable and well. No one but them can be convinced of the potential for mental healing. All illnesses and diseases can potentially result in improvement.

Those who are afflicted with bipolar disorder must ask themselves the question, "Why can't I heal mentally?" I am cognizant of the fact that any individual clinically diagnosed with bipolar disorder has the potential for being triggered mentally by a situation or an event. But as an individual who has experienced the various symptoms of manic and depressive episodes, I have had the potential of becoming mentally ill again in the far depths of my mind. What allows me to continue to experience mental healing each day is thinking about mental stability instead of sickness and depression.

Somehow, individuals who are coping with bipolar disorder must visualize a positive outcome with regard to their long-term treatment. As I previously stated in chapter 4 of this book, a depressed individual must envision mental wellness. This psychological disorder will continue to wreak havoc on the depressed individual until he or she can formulate a mental vision of healing from all of the mental agony and chaos that this mental condition brings.

One must do everything within their power to remain on a healing path mentally. Now I cannot reiterate enough how many mental health experts have unanimously concluded that an individual who is psychologically affected by bipolar disorder will not become cured of it. Though I am living with and coping with this mental disease and, in my opinion, have experienced mental healing, I cannot state for certain that I am miraculously cured.

Bipolar disorder must not be viewed as an insurmountable illness. If an individual views the illness in that way, then healing and coping will become a never-ending threat and challenge. In the life of the depressed individual, mental sickness is overcome when the individual learns how to channel wellness rather than mental torture.

Controlling one's thoughts is the key to an individual's experience of wellness. Some of those struggling with bipolar disorder must somehow develop a pattern of mind control. When it comes to thoughts that spring up within an individual's mind, there is a choice that one makes. They can choose to accept the thought or dispose of it. Mental wellness is a choice. Many who are having a difficult struggle with this mental disorder can sometimes be oblivious to those options when it comes to the way they think within their minds.

In my life, I have personally experienced how having thoughts of mental wellness has ultimately changed my mental perception of myself as well as the way that I perceive this psychological condition. Today, I do not view myself as a mentally ill individual. Instead, I envision myself as an individual who has been able to mentally heal from and cope with a mental disorder that was a part of my past.

Individuals who think about mental wellness can potentially put this mental health condition way behind them. What I mean by putting the mental health condition in their past is that they do not have to continuously struggle with it. There is mental relief from the negative thoughts that they can experience only when they are cooperative.

If you are currently taking prescribed psychotropic medicines, then I suggest that you do not cease or taper off from consuming them. Generally, this is an ongoing problem or issue for many of those in the community of bipolar bearers. The prescribed medicine does have physical side effects, but as a fellow bearer, I am confident that when the depressed individual continues to take the medicine as prescribed, without incident, then their potential for experiencing wellness in their thoughts will become more prevalent in their minds.

One must not conflict with the instructions and advice of a well-meaning and qualified doctor/therapist. Those who do are hurting their chances of sustaining long-lasting mental healing. Healing and thoughts of wellness are not typically on the mind of a depressed individual who elects not to listen and take heed to what the mental health professional is suggesting.

Many of those who follow their own path to mental wellness do not consider how the input of a psychiatrist is both vital and necessary. Though our thoughts are our own, therapists and mental health experts can help us develop the tools to formulate thoughts of wellness with positive affirmations that can be discussed during therapy sessions. Consistency in mental wellness commences when the individual believes internally that they are mentally healthy.

A positive and beautiful thing occurs when a mentally affected individual finally has thoughts of wellness. For instance, the individual's whole mood and countenance will dramatically change. Individuals who think about mental wellness are more likely to experience internal comfort.

Essentially, if any individual who is in the midst of a bipolar struggle desires to experience consistency in mental wellness, they must think positively about themselves. My suggestion to any depressed individual who is having a difficult time battling this severe mental disorder is to continue to persevere with their thoughts of mental wholeness. In the long run, I know that patience and perseverance usually pay off.

An individual who can view one's mind as an ally is also someone who will ultimately have wellness in their thoughts. For them to think about mental wellness, they must not allow themselves to wallow in pity and sorrow. This particular mindset is detrimental to the wellness process.

I am in no way suggesting that someone who is battling bipolar disorder become headstrong and so "mentally tough" that they'll have the potential to become repetitively ill. They cannot afford to become prideful and arrogant when their wellness of thoughts finally comes into fruition. Maintaining thoughts of wellness will become an ongoing battle for them, frankly, for the rest of their lives.

Some battle addiction issues daily. When it comes to an individual who is living with and coping with bipolar disorder, some may not have an addiction per se, but those who have the mental condition must also face the daily battle of potentially having negative thoughts. As I previously stated, it is common for every individual, whether mentally ill or not, to have negative thoughts sporadically.

For those who have bipolar illness, negative thoughts may consist of telling oneself, "You will never become well!" Sadly, many of those who have this particular mental disease, unfortunately, listen to the negative voice inside them. Hearing the negative influence from the voice within will, in most instances, result in this mental disorder getting the best of the depressed person. An individual who is having extreme difficulty with this psychological condition can overcome the power and mental hold that this illness brings about.

Some may be oblivious to the fact that sickness and illnesses are so powerful that these maladies become a daily fixture in the life of the affected individual. Bearers of bipolar disorder should strive to think of mental wellness instead of sickness because the mental disease will have less of a negative influence and effect.

Sufferers of this psychological condition can experience mental relief as soon as their thoughts transition from negative to positive. Thoughts of wellness and psychological comfort can become difficult for those with extreme cases of this mental disorder. Those who are in the midst of a bipolar battle and struggle must think about mental wellness to experience mental bliss as a result of having optimistic attitudes and mindsets.

After a plethora of years living with and dealing with bipolar disorder, I commence to be mentally and physically drained by the condition. There were numerous days that I felt as though my life was basically passing me by, and not in a positive way. In fact, there was a period in time when days of depression turned into months of being engulfed in mental sickness and fatigue.

I was not fatigued from doing strenuous activities that challenged me both mentally and physically. No, my tiresomeness resulted from the culmination of daily negative thoughts inside my head. Physically, because of my negative way of thinking, my entire body was on the road to other illnesses and maladies.

If you think that having a mental illness, such as bipolar disorder, only affects the mind, then you are sadly mistaken. Sometimes, individuals who are affected by this severe psychological disease are so consumed with what is going on in their minds that they tend to neglect how imperative it is to take care of themselves. For instance, not exercising, poor sleeping habits, and negative eating habits will typically result in other semblances of illnesses, such as obesity, heart disease, and diabetes.

Once other illnesses and maladies commence forming in depressed individuals, it will become difficult for them to view themselves as healthy overall. It does not require an extraordinary individual with intelligence to understand the domino effect on their mind, self-perception, and confidence when sickness consumes the whole body. Mentally fit individuals tend to be fit not only within their minds but also in other areas of their lives.

Viewing oneself as sickly does weigh heavily on one's psyche and self-image. I wholeheartedly believe that we are all who we think we are mentally. So if you think of yourself as someone who is overwhelmed by sickness and disease, then your mind will signal and relay those thoughts to other parts of your body, which can result in the shutting down and betrayal of your body.

The mental approach that I have with regard to bipolar disorder is that it is like any other health condition, which can be coped with and dealt with in a positive way when the right dosage of medicine is prescribed and when the depressed individual does not have any negative expectations. We all should not desire to live our lives each day with repetitive expectations and thoughts of sickness. Though illnesses and sicknesses will affect just about everyone at some point in their lives, it does not have to become a prevailing mindset.

A depressed individual has the potential for a life-altering positive change when their thoughts are aligned with optimism and not with the *what-ifs* of sickness, which can consume their thought process. Those who are bearers of bipolar disease must strive to obtain thoughts of mental clarity. When an individual enjoys clearance from any health concern, let alone a health condition such as bipolar disorder, wellness, not sickness, will be the determining factor.

Wholeness and wellness commence when an individual's thinking is consumed with affirmations. Mastery of these affirmations yields mental comfort and relief. For a depressed person to experience long-term consistency in mental wellness, they must first remind themselves of the positive attributes and qualities that they possess.

All individuals who have successfully battled bipolar disorder for a long time are brave and courageous. Depressed individuals are "mental warriors." The battle over their minds is both won and lost by how well they effectively envision positive thoughts of mental wellness.

Many of our goals in life began with a single thought. This is why I cannot stress enough how our thoughts are extremely important to how we can overcome a health condition or succumb to it. Individuals who have experienced some type of success in life did not acquire it immediately, in most cases.

They have to think about how to plan that particular achievement by formulating thoughts in their minds. I personally believe in the mantra that anyone can achieve anything in life only if they "put their mind into it." Bearers of bipolar disorder can think themselves into wellness. It only requires a plan, determination, and motivation to remain on the wellness spectrum of this severe psychological illness.

One must not only exercise their body to be physically fit, but the mind is also a muscle that must be worked out continuously. How does one work out the mind? It is by grooming it to become whole mentally with affirmations and positive thoughts that it will influence the individual to become a positive thinker. I have never heard of an optimistic person continuously thinking of their sickness and demise.

Once an individual is on pace to experience mental wholeness, they ultimately should thank the Creator, as well as themselves, for continually formulating positive thoughts. With the constant mental health problems that have obviously become a threat to any living being in our society, we all should strive to let our minds and thoughts consume mental wellness and stability. Some may pose the question, "How can I think about wellness when there is so much chaos in this world?" The best way to answer that question as a depressed individual is to strive to focus on the things in your life that you deem positive and beneficial to you.

If you have a loving support system, then try to relish it. Also, learn more about what contributes to a positive thought pattern in your life. Lastly, let go of any hindrance that can affect your mind and thoughts, either emotionally or psychologically.

Most individuals who can cope successfully with bipolar disorder have learned how to practice the things that I just discussed. Never become so frustrated with how difficult life may become that it somehow affects the internal wellness that you set out to accomplish. Continue to think about mental wellness and wholeness, although it may seem as though there is no progress.

Beyond the core of each depressed individual lies an individual who can deal with this psychological disorder successfully. You might be wondering how I know that. I know this fact because I am currently living in mental wellness without even thinking about the potential of becoming ill from this psychological condition ever again. My daily approach to having thoughts about mental wellness is not challenged by all the turbulence and destruction occurring within the world and society.

Personally, I acknowledge my faith in the Creator, as well as the inner confidence and vision that I developed over ten years ago that I would think of wellness each day that I am blessed enough to live. When it comes to thinking about mental wellness and wholeness, it is not a far-fetched dream. Any individual who has battled bipolar disorder can develop mental wellness.

In recent years, individuals who are afflicted with bipolar illness have been known to effectively cope with it. What I am stating in this chapter with regard to mental wellness is not an imaginary dream. Though some are experiencing difficulty with regard to thinking about mental wellness, others are successfully living and coping with the psychological disease.

A depressed individual must become mindful of how he or she has the mental power to think of consistency and sustainability with regard to bipolar disorder. Minimizing the effectiveness of medication management and intense counseling and therapy will influence an individual who suffers from the mental condition to remain in the stagnant position of mental sickness. The key to thinking about mental wellness is acknowledging that one has a psychological condition.

How can someone think about mental wellness when they are in utter denial? Some individuals who have been diagnosed with bipolar disorder do not like to admit that a mental disease is present in them. Then, suddenly, when the symptoms of their mental disorder appear, they become convinced that there is an illness of the mind. Sometimes an uncontrollable psychotic episode may help them come to terms with the mental malady.

Regardless of when they become aware of their condition, there is always an opportunity to think about mental wellness and wholeness. Once the mental condition is established and accepted by them, thoughts of mental wellness can commence. I believe that all health conditions, including bipolar disorder, should not be viewed as overbearing conditions that cause hopelessness.

Studies have proven that although this mental health disorder is prevalent in this country and throughout the world, many people think that they can become mentally well, despite what was previously believed by some mental health experts many decades ago. It is not unrealistic for any individual who is diagnosed with the bipolar disease to have hopes and thoughts of becoming well and fit mentally instead of having mental thoughts of disease and frustration.

Chapter 8

Aspire to Become a Success Story

Regaining one's mental health can become a bit of a challenge. In previous decades, it was unseen and unheard of to live consistently and successfully with bipolar disorder. This severe psychological illness was viewed by many in our culture and society as a mental illness that would ruin the life of the bearer once diagnosed.

Today, bipolar disorder does not have to be a psychological condition that can have a prolonged effect on the life of an affected individual. Though many are successfully living with and coping with this mental health illness, generally it does not equate to the road to mental redemption and recovery being easy and simple. In fact, mental illnesses, like bipolar disorder, are difficult to control initially in some severe cases.

Depressed individuals must realize that they are not the only individual in the world battling this sometimes unpredictable psychological illness. There is an adequate amount of resources available to the individual who is suffering from bipolar disorder. Mental health organizations and support groups are vital to the success of many who are mentally affected by the psychological condition.

When a depressed individual experiences support from others who are going through the same mental health crisis and overcomes the mental disease, it will have a positive effect on their life. Once one individual becomes an example of hope, other individuals who are in the midst of a bipolar struggle will be inspired. An inspired individual is also one who is internally filled with motivation and optimism.

Typically, optimism and bipolar disorder are not synonymous. This mental health condition has been associated with mental anguish and never-ending despair. It is unlikely that others who are oblivious to how the mental disease has evolved into a manageable health condition can view the psychological illness as an illness that could eventually be coped with in the long term.

I believe wholeheartedly that the mind can heal. If an individual unfortunately breaks their arm or leg, in many instances, that individual is aware that their broken bones will mend. A mentally affected individual can view their mind in the same way.

Just like any other broken part of one's body that eventually heals, the mind and the brain could also be viewed as broken and on the mend when the depressed individual experiences either a manic or depressive episode. The mentally affected person is healed in the mind and brain when he or she consistently takes the prescribed psychotropic medicine. After some time has elapsed from being on the same medication regimen, a success story can come to realization.

One must strive to defy the odds of living with bipolar disorder by never relinquishing hope that one will one day regain their mind. A person's mind can fully heal when the depressed individual gives the suggested psychotropic drug treatment a full chance. Individuals who become stories of success in dealing with bipolar disorder should always be commended.

Aspiring to become a success story when living with and coping with a psychological disorder should become the set goal. Success with anything in life requires perseverance and dedication. A depressed individual must become fully invested mentally in their psychological recovery.

Becoming a story of success when it comes to dealing with the fact that one is bipolar eventually comes down to the depressed individual. Sure, others can assist in their recovery, but in the same instance, the depressed person's supporters cannot walk in the shoes of the bearer. Recovery and success are ultimately on the shoulders of the individual with the mental condition itself.

Bipolar disorder is typically diagnosed with an intense psychological observation from a viable and board-certified psychiatrist. This particular individual, though unbiased, is the catalyst for the success story of his or her patient/and or client. The licensed psychiatrist/therapist is vital to the success and recovery of the depressed individual more than the mentally affected individual can ever realize.

Although it is never up to the psychiatrist/therapist to force their clients/patients to take the prescribed dosage of medicine each day, because of the prescribed medicine, therapy, and counseling they provide, the depressed individual can recover and improve from either a manic or depressive episode or both phases of bipolar disorder. These mental health providers, though unbiased, play a significant role in a depressed person's success story. It is due to their knowledge of how these psychotropic medicines help with the treatment and symptoms of psychiatric conditions, such as bipolar disorder, that the depressed individual is given a chance to thrive mentally and experience some semblance of normalcy in life.

My suggestion to any depressed individual who desires to become a success story with regard to effectively battling and coping with this severe mental condition is to decide within yourself that you will aggressively fight the mental disease and not become a negative statistic. Set your mind on overcoming the mental condition by remaining mentally well consistently. I know for certain that if I can become my own success story over bipolar disorder for over ten years and counting, then it is not unfathomable that another mentally affected individual cannot also do the same.

Mental success over this psychological condition does not require that the depressed individual do something out of the ordinary to acquire it. There is nothing difficult about participating in talk therapy and medication management. Identifying and recognizing negative triggers in one's life while coping with them can drastically help a depressed individual be victorious over this mental disorder. Prolonged mental success and victory depend squarely on how the sufferer of bipolar disorder is willing to consistently do what is necessary to remain on the mental health wellness path.

Proving the skeptics wrong with regard to living successfully and consistently with this severe mental illness is what many depressed individuals must aspire to. Now I am not stating that one who is afflicted with bipolar disorder should go above and beyond to silence the critics who do not believe that bipolar individuals can live a normal and full life. Bearers of this particular mental condition must never doubt the fact that they are capable of a life of bliss.

For a depressed person to have a story of success in life, they should develop their faith and confidence. True confidence does not come at the expense of others. It commences with the individual within, meaning you.

If you have a goal of sustainability in mental wellness and wholeness, do not allow anyone to deter you from accomplishing what you set out to do. Yes, you need to develop a mental vision and plan to live consistently and victoriously with this mental condition. Mental illness does not have to be a health condition that is looked upon as unbearable.

Though the world and society as a whole are declining, an individual's mental health does not have to follow that same path. Maintaining and sustaining mental stability is not as difficult as it may appear. Depressed individuals who prioritize their mental health are more likely to live successfully with their mental disorder, despite all the negative events and occurrences plaguing society.

Remaining mentally well and fit must be desired. With all of the catastrophes and tragic events occurring each day, it is easy for one to neglect the need to maintain mental wellness. Some have decided to allow all of the negative issues that are prevalent in this world to influence and dictate how they should feel mentally.

Millions of people have bipolar disorder, but out of all of them, I am curious to know how these particular individuals are really feeling mentally and internally. Sometimes others who are not as supportive of those who are suffering from mental illnesses, such as bipolar disorder, have a psychological and negative effect on the individual. It is due to this negative influence in the mind of a depressed individual that many do not desire to improve mentally from the psychological nightmare this mental disorder poses.

No bearer of this severe psychological disorder should continue to have the mindset of a victim. Individuals with that attitude and mindset cannot develop a life of mental success and consistency. Instead, they continue to live a life of pity and stagnation.

A life of mental stagnation definitely hinders the depressed individual's progress toward becoming mentally whole and successful. First, the mentally affected person must realize that their mental improvement is only impeded because of the individual's lack of motivation to remain mentally well. Living with and coping successfully with bipolar disorder commences and ends with the depressed individual's determination and drive.

Graduating from mental despair to successfully living with bipolar disorder is definitely possible and attainable. One has to continue to build upon the process of acquiring mental success. A depressed individual can do this when they realize that their goal of mental stability is never out of reach.

In the genesis of my mental health journey and battle with bipolar disorder, I never could have imagined how I would one day be on the mental wellness path. For years, my bipolar struggle was difficult to navigate. Though I never attempted suicide, I can recall a dark period in my experience with this psychological condition in which I felt hopeless and unmotivated to even rise from my bed in the morning.

Some are oblivious to the fact that, in many instances, a success story does not commence with success. It usually derives from pain and is the antithesis of prosperity in a given situation or circumstance. Any individual who experiences real success in life will remember the lean times with regard to their successful journey.

The road to mental success is sometimes long and tedious. It is a journey that can have many roadblocks and detours. When this occurs, a depressed person has to decide whether or not to persevere on the mental wellness path and journey or allow the detour to negatively affect them.

What I mean by a mental detour is that the mentally affected individual can experience a setback mentally. They can be hospitalized and treated for the mental health condition, or they can become emotionally triggered again. If these scenarios do occur, one should not lose hope that one can potentially live each day with mental health success.

One key to continuous mental wellness is perseverance. An individual will not win the bipolar battle without developing a persistent attitude and mindset. So what if you just happen to experience another episode or bout with this mental disorder? It does not mean that you are a failure.

In fact, when it comes to anyone being a failure in anything in life, the individual who does not try is essentially unsuccessful. Those who are having difficulty in their battle with bipolar disorder must continue to persevere in hopes of sustaining mental stability. I believe that perseverance in the midst of my bipolar struggle and battle has kept me grounded and appreciative of where I am now when it comes to experiencing prolonged mental wellness.

Just because an individual is blessed enough to become victorious and successful in the battle over bipolar disorder does not mean that they can relax and have an arrogant and complacent mindset. The battle and struggle over mental wellness and stability are continuous. Successfully overcoming and coping with this psychological disease means that the mentally affected individual is living their life day to day without the mental disease wreaking havoc on their quest to become mentally stable.

True success with this psychological disorder comes when the depressed individual thrives and remains alive. Achieving success in bipolar disorder occurs when the mentally affected individual is joyful and content. The life of an individual who is in the midst of a manic or depressive episode can be challenging.

Some may not foresee living successfully with this severe mental condition because of the mental agony that can result from it. When a depressed individual is in deep depression, they might lose their will to live. Success over the mental disease is not on the mind of an individual who desires not to be a valued member of life.

Individuals who are having mental health challenges because of bipolar disorder must somehow learn how to appreciate being among the living. I am personally cognizant of how life is sometimes cruel and lonely. Many people who have that attitude and mindset must not try to deal with feelings of loneliness and abandonment alone.

A depressed individual should seek out help from those who will empathize with and understand how they feel. When a mentally affected individual is fortunate enough to discover mental health organizations and support groups that are like-minded, that individual who was on the brink of ending their life can finally be mentally well and whole again. Real success over bipolar disorder comes when the depressed individual can leave those feelings of abandonment and loneliness in the past.

In this sometimes difficult world, it might seem as though unhappiness and sorrow will always prevail. An individual who is in a state of depression may have the attitude and mental mindset that no one else cares about them. This world is huge.

Billions of people collectively make up this world. I can confidently state that at least one person can relate to an individual who is in a state of mental anguish and turmoil. Those who feel agony and mental chaos from bipolar disorder can overcome how they are currently feeling.

Emotions and mental perceptions can gradually change. This is why I believe that an individual who is struggling mentally today can eventually thrive tomorrow. If depressed individuals can develop optimism and hope over a substantial amount of time, then they are deemed mentally successful.

Once a mentally affected individual regains a positive attitude and mindset, the journey to mental success is accomplished. Though the journey to mental success is ultimately realized, this does not mean that the individual's mental recovery should come to a halt. Real success in severe psychological illness occurs when the depressed individual is in a positive mental headspace.

Most individuals who are successful in life are focused and consistent mentally. If a depressed individual desires to maintain a consistent level of mental stability, that individual must also become laser-focused on their mental recovery and health. When a depressed person can live their life without becoming mentally inhibited, then a success story with regard to overcoming this psychological condition is definitely in the individual's future.

Stories of mental success have become more prevalent in recent years. Medication, therapy, and support have been significant factors in the mentally affected individual's victory. A depressed individual has a greater chance of mental sustainability when all of those factors are working simultaneously in their lives.

Individuals with bipolar disease must not view themselves as inferior or mentally deficient. When a mentally affected individual has an inferiority complex, they will generally not be able to set goals or have the same dreams as those who are not mentally affected. Just because one has bipolar disorder does not mean that they should set limitations on what can be achieved in life.

For depressed individuals, they must adopt the mentality that they are not the mental illness or disease. They have to avoid labeling themselves to accomplish those goals in life that some suggest cannot be accomplished because of a mental disorder. No depressed individual should wait on others to write their story of mental success.

Instead, they should do all the things in life that their hearts desire and that are within reason. As I previously stated in an earlier chapter, bipolar disorder is not just a mental disorder that affects the brain; it is also a disorder that can drastically affect mood. It has been revealed in the past that many sufferers of this mood and mental disorder are typically intelligent and creative. This explains why many people can accomplish just about anything in life because of their mental capabilities. In other words, there are infinite possibilities for them if only they believe in their minds and hearts that their set dreams and goals are definitely attainable. In my opinion, they should be open to success both mentally and physically.

From a mental perspective, as I have been discussing all along, mental success is obtained when the bearer of the mental illness becomes receptive to the various methods that influence mental stability. Achieving physical success is when an individual physically does the activity to accomplish it. For example, finishing college or acquiring one's dream job requires some type of physical activity.

One cannot complete college or discover their career path without becoming physically active. If an individual desires to graduate from a college or university, that individual must become physically committed to attending class regularly while physically completing the work that is required. As far as achieving success with regard to one's career path, the individual must physically interview for the job and formulate a resume, which requires the individual to physically type it. Regardless of how physical success in life is achieved by a mentally affected person, it will always stem from the individual's mental perception and perspective.

Depressed individuals are most likely to continue to have mental success over bipolar disorder when they have some semblance of support. This mental condition cannot be coped with on the individual's own. Individuals who are living with bipolar illness are more equipped to have mental consistency when a supportive friend or loved one does not lose faith that the depressed individual can eventually improve psychologically.

Hopefully, bearers of the mental disease can share their success stories with those who continued to persevere through this unpredictable psychological disorder. In my life, my mother has been supporting me through this mental condition since its onset. There were times when this mental disorder negatively affected my life in the midst of manic and depressive episodes.

Because of the negative symptoms I experienced as a result of this severe mental illness, many of my personal relationships commence to suffer. While I was at that low point in my life, my mother was the only one who never gave up hope in my potential to overcome this mental disease. She always told me that my condition would eventually improve, although I did not share that same positive outlook.

An individual who has dealt with bipolar disorder for a long time cannot boast about having pristine mental health until the psychological illness is not a continuous topic of discussion. When this mental disorder becomes less of an issue in the depressed person's life, then the individual is on their way to becoming a story of mental success. I believe that most individuals who are suffering from bipolar disorder would love to see others who have coped with the illness successfully, despite the adversities and challenges that this psychological disease causes.

This mental health condition can affect the affected individual in two ways. The first way is when the individual does not desire to improve and views life from a pessimistic perspective. Another way—and the best way—is the individual's will and need to combat and fight through the illness's mental grasp.

I am aware of the fact that when a depressed individual develops the desire to fight this lifelong mental battle, it will usually commence when their support system somehow motivates them to continue to press on in life. Bipolar disorder cannot defeat the individual who decides to battle the disorder with all of their mind and heart. There is always the potential for a mental health breakthrough.

Success in the life of a depressed person is not always easy to sustain. Though mental consistency is at times difficult to acquire, it is not something unrealistic for the individual who desires to achieve mental health success. Consistency in support is imperative for the bearer's mental aspirations.

Self-love is vital to one's mental success. When an individual loves themselves, they will take all of the necessary precautions to continue self-care. Self-care is what ultimately leads to mental health success and prosperity.

We all need self-love to experience the challenges of life. Bipolar disorder is a mental health challenge that can diminish self-love. Some of those who are in the midst of the mental battle may lose the need to have a love for themselves, thus negatively affecting their potential for mental bliss and consistency.

Depressed individuals must somehow recognize that they have the power to change their mental health narrative. Once mentally affected individuals discover their true mental core and power, they can rewrite what they initially thought of themselves after being diagnosed with this mental illness. The question of successfully coping with bipolar disorder should not be, "Can I cope and combat this mental health battle?" One should always answer that question with, "I will combat and overcome this mental health struggle with the help of my Creator, my support system, and myself."

Many of those who are battling with bipolar disorder sometimes blame themselves for having the psychological illness. No one is to blame for their brain not functioning at its optimum level, which typically results in the illness' symptoms. In most cases, blaming oneself or others will have a prolonged negative psychological effect, which can manifest itself into resentment and bitterness.

The chance of writing a narrative of mental success over bipolar disorder decreases when the mentally affected individual is wallowing in negative attitudes and mindsets. If this describes you, the reader, then I challenge you to no longer live your life looking to discover the origin of your mental health struggles but to strive to dedicate your time and life to embrace the solution to this psychological disorder. Most depressed people are oblivious to the fact that their positive or negative perceptions about how they view bipolar disorder are the determining and contributing factors in whether they will be able to become a success story and part of the solution or dwell on the negative factors and be part of the problem in terms of continual mental wellness.

Not cooperating with one's psychiatrist/therapist and having the mindset that their way is best for coping with bipolar disorder are just a few ways that a depressed individual negatively contributes to becoming the source of their prolonged mental health problems and issues. I believe that this is also an example of their self-sabotaging their own mental health treatment and plan. Before any depressed person eventually claims victory over this severe mental health condition, they must first exhaust all options.

What I mean by exhausting one's options is for the depressed individual to follow up with their mental health treatment. Resistance to the plan and treatment of a licensed and board-certified psychiatrist is what ultimately affects the affected individual's plan to have continuous mental health success. It is better to not resist what their psychiatrists/therapists suggest if they want to turn their mental health journey around.

Your success over this psychological condition should not be defined by the standards of others. Each individual who has been in the midst of a bipolar battle is different. Although many of those who are afflicted with bipolar disorder have varying paths to mental wellness, most depressed individuals have the common goal of sustaining their mental health.

All who are battling bipolar illness have the potential to write their own mental health story. First, acceptance of one's mental illness must be established for them to experience a mental comeback. Coming back from a severe mental disorder is difficult but also possible.

My own comeback path into mental health and wholeness was not always smooth. I will never state to anyone that my recovery from bipolar disorder did not have its share of "bumps in the road." There were times that I thought to myself that I would never be able to experience mental consistency. That was approximately fifteen years ago. As a depressed individual, it took a while for me to write my success story over this mental condition. Just like I previously stated, I am probably the last person one would think would be living in continuous mental health bliss.

I made numerous failed attempts to maintain my mental wellness. You might be thinking, *What changed for him?* In my opinion, this might sound cliché, but what ultimately helped in my mental recovery were faith, hope, and optimism. When I was last hospitalized, I vowed to myself that I would change my mental approach with regard to this psychological disorder.

Voila! Changing my mental perception and perspective became the catalyst for my mental health story. For example, in previous years, I viewed bipolar disorder as a mental disorder that was solely responsible for ruining my life. It is due to that mindset that I gave the psychological disease dominion and control.

Bipolar disorder controlled my mind for many years before I was able to finally combat it with the right treatment and a positive attitude. Many bearers of the psychological disease can also enjoy mental recovery. For depressed individuals to experience mental wellness for years to come, they must learn how to listen and not become difficult and stubborn when being treated for their mental condition.

Some of those who are mentally affected by this severe mental illness cannot fathom how they could mentally thrive, although they are battling racing thoughts, sadness, and hopelessness. The one thing that I can state for a fact is that bipolar disorder does not have to result in a sad story. A depressed individual has the mental power and control to eventually change the course of their mental trajectory when they view the psychological illness as a health condition that does not have to mentally affect their entire lifetime.

Long-lasting mental success is definitely not far out of reach for a bipolar individual. Others may not celebrate your mental recovery, but only you know how far you have come mentally. Mental consistency and recovery are the results of a successful narrative.

As a culture and society, we all love the story of a comeback. Bipolar disorder is a mental illness that leaves no other choice but to make a comeback mentally. Depressed individuals who come back from this severe mental disorder are resilient.

This is an attribute that many of those who are in the midst of the bipolar struggle should strive to acquire. Coping with and living a life of mental success are not as difficult as they may seem. Initially, coping with bipolar disorder may not equate to resiliency, but after dealing with the extreme mood levels of the psychological condition, one can concur that becoming resilient is necessary.

Mental resilience and recovery will only come to fruition when the depressed person is motivated and patient. Yes, they must become determined to fight through all of the setbacks and negative occurrences that can result from having this mental condition. Once they overcome all of the times that bipolar disorder has affected their lives in some way, they can inspire themselves.

When I reflect on all of my psychological struggles and battles with this severe mental health disease throughout my life, I cannot avoid the fact that I have somehow been fortunate enough to survive and remain alive. Each day, millions are suffering from bipolar disorder and do not know which way to turn or where to seek help. If they are courageous enough to realize that something is not right with them mentally and they desire to know what is wrong, then that is the first step to formulating the path to mental recovery.

We all have aspirations and dreams in life. Some are more prone to realizing those dreams and goals because they will not allow anyone or anything to hinder their plans to achieve them. With regard to a bearer of bipolar disorder, they should always aspire to overcome the symptoms of the disorder to become an example of mental health prosperity.

Prospering in anything in life, typically, is synonymous with an individual flourishing and thriving. It is the epitome of success. With some semblance of success, generally, the outcome is positive.

Bearers of bipolar disorder who have learned how to cope and thrive in this cruel world have true stories of success. In the past, an individual who was diagnosed with this psychological disorder could not imagine how they would thrive in life while trying to manage a mental illness. Currently, with advancements in research and treatments, those who are diagnosed can become a mental health success story.

— *Chapter 9* —

Embrace the Process

Anything that one does to become successful in life requires a process. Individuals who are living with bipolar disorder must strive to go along with all of the steps required to become mentally well. Now I am cognizant of the fact that, for some, the process of remaining mentally consistent is sometimes difficult.

It is not always easy to take prescribed psychotropic medicine at the same time each day. But if taking the prescribed medicine will help the depressed individual maintain consistency in their mood and mind, then the process is definitely worthwhile. It takes a village to remain mentally fit consistently.

The village for the mentally affected individual consists of their psychiatrist/therapist and support system. Coping with bipolar disorder is more than just medication management. Though it is a vital part of the mental health process, the depressed individual's village also plays a significant role.

If a mentally affected individual does not embrace the process when it comes to living and coping successfully with bipolar disorder, then they will have a lesser chance of sustaining mental wellness. There are no shortcuts for them to develop consistency over this psychological illness. This is the sole reason they must continue to exercise patience.

Most psychologically affected individuals may become oblivious to how imperative it is to not deviate from the daily process of taking the prescribed medicine, eating healthy, exercising, and getting the appropriate amount of rest each night. I can honestly state with confidence that when I decided to incorporate those things into my daily routine, my mental health commenced to improve. Every depressed person should expect to experience recovery in their mental state when the process of remaining mentally fit is taken seriously.

A depressed individual must be willing to see the process through to remain mentally stable. Initially, the process of mental stabilization may seem dull. But in due time, the daily process and regimen will eventually pay off.

As a fellow sufferer of bipolar disorder, I have learned how to trust the daily process I commit to consistently. Because I wholeheartedly trust and believe in all the things that I am doing to remain mentally well, I now credit my process and daily routine for allowing me to enjoy mental stability for a plethora of years. The only requirement that I would suggest to any mentally affected individual is to continue to persevere and be committed to all that the process requires and entails to remain mentally consistent.

For any individual to enjoy any type of success in life, they must also commit to the entire process. Bearers of bipolar disorder should also commit themselves to the process regimen. Successful living for the bearer is only established with their full commitment to the process of long-lasting mental stability.

Before any individual can become consistent in their mental health success, the depressed individual needs to continue to have faith in the process to remain mentally whole and fit. Without belief, the depressed person's mental condition will remain in the same stagnant state. I believe that those who continuously rebel against the process of developing mental wellness are essentially becoming their own worst enemies.

The worst thing that a mentally affected individual can do is become a detriment to themselves. This is what occurs when the process of remaining mentally stable is either abandoned or not fully embraced. Many lack the discipline to maintain a daily routine.

Routines require the individual to have self-motivation. It can become quite a task for some to become "self-starters." Instead, they experience codependence.

A goal for all individuals who have bipolar disease is to become as independent and self-sufficient as possible. How do they become mentally functioning individuals? First, they must become receptive to the process of developing the tools to mentally cope with the world. Also, they must understand how the process of becoming able to deal with the lack of empathy from some in our society who still label and stigmatize members of the mentally ill community is long and sometimes difficult to bear.

For someone to move forward in life, especially if he or she has a mental condition, such as bipolar disorder, they must not have feelings and emotions of fear. Some in this life can overcome fear through trial and error. For some depressed individuals, the way that fear is minimized is solely based on the counseling and therapeutic process.

Ultimately, when an individual affected by bipolar disorder or any other mental illness learns how to cope successfully with their illness, with themselves, and with the world, then there is the potential for them to become mentally strong. A strong mind is essentially an effective one. Once the mind becomes powerful, then the process of mental wellness should be valued.

Are you valuing the mental wellness process? If one somehow appreciates the process of becoming whole mentally, then their entire mood and demeanor will blossom. Overall wellness is derived from having an optimistic viewpoint, which equates to the mind and body also thriving in wellness. We, as humans, are creatures of the process of habit.

Developing mental habits that are void of fear and worry is acquired over time. Time usually consists of processes and sequences. In other words, a depressed individual cannot learn how to cope with emotional and mental triggers without the process of time and progression working in an orderly manner.

Hope in the process of remaining mentally fit and whole is extremely imperative. Without some semblance of optimism, the depressed individual is just going through the motions. No individual can maintain a consistent level of hope with regard to coping successfully with this psychological disease if the process is not embraced.

Bipolar disorder is combated victoriously when the mentally affected individual is willing to take a risk. What I mean by taking a chance with regard to their mental wellness is that they must somehow trust and accept that the process of going to therapy, taking the prescribed psychotropic medication, and recognizing and coping with emotional triggers are the only ways that they can discover prolonged success over this psychological disorder. We can all hope for a brighter tomorrow when the process of remaining mentally stable and well is wholeheartedly accepted.

As a depressed individual myself, I commenced to make a turn for the better when it came to coping with bipolar disorder the very minute I decided to trust that the process would allow me to remain mentally well by not viewing it as a hindrance but as beneficial. It is more likely than not that some who are battling with bipolar disorder would prefer not to take the prescribed psychotropic medicine or receive therapy treatment continuously. In reality, there is no other alternative method they can use if they desire to experience prolonged mental health success.

Personally, I do not think that individuals who are in the midst of a bipolar struggle have any other option but to have hope that their mental health condition will significantly improve. The mistake that many commit with regard to mental health improvement is disregarding the mental health process once they become better mentally. Once depressed individuals discover all that contributes to good mental health, I highly recommend that they continue to do those same things while never relinquishing their hope.

An optimistic and hopeful attitude toward the process of remaining mentally stable and consistent is what many psychiatrists and therapists strive to influence their patients/clients to have when coping with a severe mental illness, such as bipolar disorder. The depressed individual must realize that the process of mental stabilization is not there to cause harm. In fact, the process is there to help the depressed individual improve and have mental discipline.

In most cases, the prescribed medicine, counseling, and therapy will result in the depressed individual eventually transforming into a productive and reliable member of society. A bearer of bipolar disorder does not become an optimistic and hopeful human being without welcoming each process with open arms to continue on their mental success journey. There is a life of consistency in mental health success when people are receptive to the lifelong process of mental wellness without an attitude of rebellion.

Feelings of joy can be experienced when an individual's life is in order. No one can have sustainable happiness without loving their life or being content. The bearer of bipolar disorder can also experience satisfaction in life.

You might be asking how I know this. I know that depressed individuals have the potential for lifelong contentment when they allow themselves to become comfortable with the mental health process. The process of enjoying mental consistency should not be fought "tooth and nail." If the process is looked upon in that way, then a negative attitude will ensue.

This world and society are in the process of decline in every way imaginable. In many cases, when it comes to all of the processes in life, change and evolution are at the center of them. All living beings are in the process of evolving.

Some have evolved in the process of life by being mentally and emotionally wounded by events and circumstances that had a negative effect on them. Most individuals who are affected by bipolar disorder have encountered something in their lives that triggered either a manic or depressive episode, or both in some instances. Now I am not a licensed psychiatrist or therapist, but coming from experience as well as dealing with others who have the same mental condition, I am aware that an individual's life experiences and environment contribute enormously to the individual having a psychotic episode, although hereditary and genes are also factors.

With regard to one having the bipolar condition, either the depressed person is in the process of a sharp mental decline or is progressing into an improved mental state. I believe that they must make an internal decision, which can significantly impact their whole mental outlook on themselves and the world. A decision about whether to accept the process of mental and psychological decline or strive to somehow overcome mental adversity must be made.

Honesty is vital to the process of the bearer of any health condition. Those who suffer from bipolar disorder are not exempt from a frank assessment of their mental condition and the current state of their lives. If they are honest with themselves, then they can conclude that they are in the process of a psychological decline.

Nothing positive can come from any depressed person improving when they are not embracing their truth. The truth is for them to identify that they are far from experiencing mental wellness. Once the truth is established, the process of becoming mentally well and whole will be greatly appreciated.

Viewing the mental health process as a win-win situation is vital for an individual who has struggled with bipolar illness. There is nothing that would result in the bearer being a loser in the quest for mental wellness when the process is totally embraced. They can only be defeated when they purposely sabotage their mental health growth.

Some may disagree that all that encompasses mental health success is not an actual process. To some, there is no validity in doing the whole mental health process, which was previously described. I can state for certain that the same individuals who believe that the process to become mentally whole and fit is not valid are the same individuals who do not have any clue about the amount of hard work and dedication required for them to experience mental health relief.

At the end of the day, the mentally affected individual does not have to become concerned about whether or not their process with regard to mental recovery needs any type of validity to others who can never comprehend the mental struggle. There is more to mental stability than just taking pills. Sure, the right psychotropic medicine assists with the process, but the process of the mentally affected individual becoming confident and comfortable with their condition is crucial to the process of healing.

In the genesis of my psychological battle with the mental condition, I naively thought that there was no method or process to mental healing and recovery. Of course, I did not realize that I was ultimately one of the reasons I had a chance to recover mentally. When it comes to the healing process, any individual who is in the midst of a battle for recovery must make a lifestyle sacrifice.

For some, this can prove difficult. Many of us do not like to sacrifice anything in life, especially if it affects having fun with others or doing activities that we love and are familiar with. Individuals who are diagnosed with bipolar disorder and enjoy drinking and being in an atmosphere where their mental health recovery can be affected and threatened are essentially disregarding the process. Indulging in any type of alcohol or chemical substances for the mentally affected individual is basically a lose-lose situation.

Included in a depressed individual's process of mental recovery is the sacrifice of not engaging in any kind of alcoholic consumption or mind-altering chemical substances. A sufferer of bipolar disorder has a greater chance of mental stabilization and consistency when the process and sacrifice to avoid those specific substances are realized. A mind that is free from any kind of chemical influence other than the prescribed medicine is a mind that will thrive and prosper. If the individual who is living with this psychological disease can embrace the process and make sacrifices, then the road to becoming mentally stable for a long time will be in full sight.

Seeing one's mental health recovery blossom into full existence is exciting and satisfying. This is the gift that is the result of days, months, and even years of sacrifice and patience. Many in our society do not have the patience to realize anything in life.

We are in a world and culture of instant gratification and ready-made products. I can fully understand why any kind of process can become challenging for the average person. As a nation and culture familiar with receiving almost anything with the touch of a button or a snap of a finger, many may conclude that most processes in life take entirely too long.

Hopefully, one will have their whole life ahead of him or her. Realistically, no one can be assured of the near future. Somehow, an individual must allow oneself to live one day at a time.

When someone can live the life process with that approach, then living successfully with a mental disorder is not as difficult. A depressed individual must break down the twenty-four-hour period in a day into increments. Once the individual has the incremented process down, he or she can practice a disciplined daily routine.

I am also cognizant of the fact that incremented days are subject to change. This is because life today is so unpredictable. With the help of a schedule, depressed individuals can basically train their mind and body to have some type of purpose to honor that daily task.

As humans, we all need to have a purpose to live out each day. If one's purpose for living is not realized, then the process of living becomes stagnant and suffers. Those who are mentally affected by bipolar disorder must not view the process of living as dull and boring.

There is so much in a given day that can be life-changing in a positive and significant way. Depressed individuals should strive to enjoy the process of living despite its uncertainty. Although the times in which we live are becoming increasingly difficult by the day, it still does not negate the fact that life is still a never-ending process.

Life should not only be lived each day, but a mentally affected individual should also view their life as a continuous process of mental health progression and ultimately successful living. For a bearer of the bipolar condition to have lifelong mental recovery and success, they must not view their illness in the same way society would. Instead, they should view their mental health progress as a steady climb.

The process of achieving mental health success is lifelong. Depressed individuals must mentally prepare themselves to reclaim their mind again. Though there might be challenging days ahead, the process of becoming mentally whole will not change. Individuals who desire to live successfully and cope with the whole process of mental wellness must never overlook its importance.

Cherishing the mental health process to regain mental sustainability is definitely needed in the life of the mentally affected individual. When they cherish something in life, they will typically hold that person or item close to them. With regard to mental health, a depressed individual must also cherish the fact that there is a potential to experience mental wellness when the process is accepted and desired.

I love facing each day with anticipation and contentment. It is due to my newfound mindset to hold and cherish the mental health process that I can have hope and optimism for tomorrow. If the mental health process is helping the bearer of bipolar disorder to live every day in mental wellness, then it is imperative that the process be embraced and cherished.

Because I personally cherish my mental health stability, I will not put myself in a position or situation that will negatively affect my mental health process. When the process of remaining relatively mentally fit and whole is desired, that individual will go above and beyond to sustain it. One who cherishes their mental health will experience prolonged mental consistency.

Some individuals who are living with and coping with bipolar illness do not put in the effort to become mentally whole and well. Instead, these same individuals are reckless with regard to their mental health and recovery. For example, some are not prioritizing the process of mental wellness by having a lackadaisical attitude.

How can they not prioritize their recovery? Perhaps denial and a lack of confidence in their mental condition improving are significant factors. One must believe wholeheartedly in their mind and heart that the mental health process will inevitably help them. One must understand that cherishing and embracing the process of mental stabilization is the only way that a depressed individual will have any chance to defy the prognosis and regain their mental health.

There is peace of mind for the mentally affected individual who has learned how to cherish and embrace the process of mental recovery. This is the goal that all individuals afflicted with bipolar disease must continue to strive for. Mental wellness and peace of mind occur when the mental health process is wholeheartedly embraced.

All depressed individuals in the midst of a bipolar battle have the potential to experience mental bliss. They do not have to live their lives in misery and disarray. He or she can eventually experience mental recovery and wellness when the quest to maintain mental stability is not viewed as a tremendous challenge.

The life of a bipolar individual will never be perfect. Others' lives are also far from flawless. They have a chance to experience a life filled with an adequate amount of peace and joy when the mental health process becomes their priority.

Prioritizing mental recovery is what is needed in the life of the bipolar bearer. In today's society, the mental health of every individual is becoming more important. The world as a whole is struggling to remain mentally stable, especially when you factor in all of the tragic and negative occurrences that have plagued it.

Good-quality mental health care should be available to all because of the ongoing mental stress experienced by many. It is not unusual for anyone to develop a mental illness, such as bipolar disorder. Once someone is initially diagnosed with the mental health disorder, the process of becoming mentally whole again must immediately commence.

A depressed individual should never tackle this mental disease on their own. Previously, I discussed how imperative it is to not only trust the process of mental health recovery but that the bearer of the psychological illness must also embrace the village. The village, which consists of the psychiatrist and the mentally affected individual's support system, should hold the individual accountable.

What I mean by accountability is that the village must not allow the depressed individual to wallow in mental pity or frustration when the process becomes overwhelming, difficult, and unbearable. I am cognizant of the fact that it is not always simple and easy to have a positive attitude and mindset when one's mind is either filled with anxiety or in the deep depths of depression.

If the sufferer of bipolar disorder does not have some semblance of a mental health process, then sadly, their mental health will not improve, or even worse, they may not be a willing participant in their own mental recovery. The common denominator in their mental stability is them. This is why the mentally affected individual must always become involved in their mental health process in some way.

Valuing mental wellness is not others' responsibility. A psychologically affected individual must put forth an "all-out" effort to be mentally stable. Although they may have more than enough members of their village, ultimately, the village members cannot do the mental health process themselves.

Most of us have taken the test for our driver's license. In the driving portion of the test, no one but the individual who is driving can take it. Though the individual's parents may have taught them to drive, the parents cannot take the driver's test for them.

A process must be taken for the individual to receive his or her driver's license. The written portion of the driver's test is just as vital as the road test. In both instances, the individual is mainly responsible for either failing the whole driver's test or successfully passing it. This same kind of scenario can be applied to an individual who is in the process of mental recovery. In other words, the road to success is complete when the individual's responsibility is assumed.

The impact of an embraced mental health process is enormous. A positive mood and demeanor are the result of following through on one's recovery. After years of sustaining the daily process of remaining mentally stable, the bearer of bipolar disorder will view themselves as someone who is consistent and can cope successfully with a psychological disorder.

Bipolar disorder is best overcome when one is consistent in their daily process of maintaining their mental care. No depressed individual should rebel against doing all the things on a day-to-day basis to help themselves become the best person they can be. If the mental health process is not well received, then the end result can be detrimental to the mentally affected individual's life and the lives of those close to them.

Every daily process that individuals with the psychological disease perform to develop mental consistency is not in vain. Some of those who are in the bipolar community do not see any need to continuously maintain mental discipline with regard to having an ongoing process to recover mentally. Mental discipline is needed for mental recovery to be successful for a substantial amount of time.

Ultimately, mental consistency over bipolar disorder is experienced by the depressed individual in due time. When the process of mental recovery is embraced, the bearer can eventually be someone who will have happiness. To enjoy any kind of consistency in happiness, an individual must love their life.

Individuals affected by this psychological condition can experience just as much joy and contentment in life as those who are not affected. First, the depressed person must not deviate from their regular mental health routine and regimen. The process of remaining mentally fit and whole should always be appreciated and valued.

What can a depressed person do to remain convinced that the process of mental health recovery really does work? One thing that they can do is look at the mental success of others who have the same condition and are still mentally stable. I believe that the successful bearers of bipolar disorder will become willing to share how they acquired that mental success. Also, I can bet a "pretty penny" that those who basked in their mental stability and recovery would suggest to others that mental discipline and carrying out the daily process to sustain mental health were possible only because they had faith and belief that the process would work.

Mental health and self-care are continuous processes that every individual, including those who are afflicted with this psychological condition, must strive to embrace every day of their lives. Once the mentally affected individual becomes cognizant of their psychological improvement, mental recovery can be viewed as a beautiful process of healing. A healed mind is a mind that has been challenged by the process required to experience mental victory.

Trusting and embracing the process of being mentally well and whole again is what has to happen in the life of an individual who is battling bipolar disorder. The battle over their mental stability will turn out to be an "all-out war and nightmare" when the process of becoming mentally stable is undervalued. A mental health condition, such as bipolar disorder, is won when the process becomes the affected individual's primary focus.

Embracing the process of mental recovery does require that the depressed individual and their support system wholeheartedly participate and cooperate with what the process suggests to remain mentally whole. There should not be anything that the bearer of the condition should be focused on other than how to heal mentally. I am fully aware that the process of remaining mentally stable can be repetitive and tedious.

Most individuals who are coping with bipolar disorder daily will not always enjoy the daily sacrifice required of them. For them not to experience any mental setbacks, they do not have any other alternative but to trust that the daily dosage of medicine, journaling, and remaining focused on their mental health will greatly help them live a life that is not predicated on this mental disorder.

Becoming open to the process of mental healing is the first and really the only step that one should take if one desires to live their life without the psychological condition taking full reign over their life. People can tell someone to act and think positively every day, but they neglect to tell someone how to discover and maintain it. This proves true in the life of someone who is battling bipolar illness.

Individuals who encounter manic or depressive episodes cannot only be told to have a positive and consistent mood. They have to learn how to navigate through this life of unpredictability and uncertainty with sometimes uncontrollable moods and mental disorders. Although an individual who is living and coping with bipolar disorder cannot pinpoint if and when they will become emotionally and mentally triggered by some event or traumatic occurrence, the process and tools that are learned by talking with one's psychiatrist and support groups will always be a viable source for their lifelong mental recovery.

Many mental health professionals and experts concur that the process of mental health recovery never ceases to end. As a depressed individual, I believe that every individual is susceptible to experiencing some battle with some type of mental health issue. The process of remaining mentally whole and stable must never be frowned upon.

Every individual who is coping with and living with bipolar disorder or any other type of mental illness has a choice about whether the process is something that they will embrace or view as a nuisance. If one views the mental process and recovery as a nuisance, then the chance of that individual becoming mentally successful decreases or diminishes. One must embrace the process of mental healing and recovery because it gives them the best chance for prolonged relief and joy.

—— *Chapter 10* ——

Coping Successfully with Bipolar

Successful living with bipolar disorder commences with a positive vision of lifelong mental wellness. This mental health disorder can easily be coped with successfully if the depressed individual is willing to follow all of the advice and instructions of a licensed psychiatrist or therapist. Mental illnesses, like bipolar disorder, are successfully treated with medication and therapy.

When the illness is properly treated, the mentally affected individual does not have to constantly worry about their mental health. Instead, they can potentially live their lives without fear of either a manic or depressive episode. I believe that a bipolar individual has just as much of a chance of joy and happiness as any other individual who is not affected by bipolar illness.

Realistically, coping with bipolar disorder is definitely obtainable. With all of the advancements in mental health treatments and the development of tools and techniques to help assist the individual who may be emotionally triggered, this particular psychological condition does not have to result in the demise of the bearer. Living with and coping successfully with this mental disorder means that the depressed individual can begin a new day without experiencing any of the negative symptoms of the psychological disease.

Regaining one's mental health should be the goal of any mentally affected individual who has previously struggled with this severe mental illness. Before any depressed person can experience mental success, in many instances, they will experience mental woes. Bipolar disorder is a mental health condition that is not always easy to treat.

Discovering the right psychotropic medicine and the right amount of dosage to take can be a bit of a challenge for the doctor and the client/patient. It is imperative that a mentally affected individual be both participatory and vocal when it comes to their treatment. They must strive to take a mental inventory of their treatment if they can do so.

A mental inventory will most likely lead the depressed person to become more familiar with their own psychological state. Assessing one's mental health is one of the ways that individuals with psychological illness can gauge where they are with regard to whether they are mentally well enough to cope. The process of coping successfully with bipolar disorder should never become burdensome.

Simply taking the prescribed psychotropic medicine and continuously assessing one's mental state are key factors in coping successfully with bipolar disorder, but the bearer must also not have feelings of denial. Although I do believe in the divine healing of the Almighty, I am also not willing to relinquish the process vital to my own mental health improvement. In most cases of prolonged treatment success of mental health, the affected individual can persevere by realizing the importance of how the daily routine and regimen are effective in achieving success.

Balancing one's mood is essential to coping with bipolar disorder. This psychological illness cannot be successfully coped with when the affected individual's mood is unbalanced and out of sorts. Mental stabilization is needed if the depressed individual intends to thrive mentally.

An individual whose mood is balanced can receive potentially unfavorable news without being too emotional. Now I am not in any way stating that any individual who receives devastating news should not experience any type of emotion. As humans, we are all considered emotional beings.

With regard to an individual who suffers from bipolar disorder, emotions can, in many cases, fuel an episode. Emotions can be a sensitive topic for someone who is in the midst of a bipolar battle. They can experience the emotions of life, but the emotions will not have a long-lasting effect on them.

As a depressed individual, I can honestly state that I am not controlled by my mood and emotions. Though my emotions are not the determining factor in my daily mood, that does not mean that I cannot feel empathy or emotional pain at times. Some events that I hear on the evening news can inspire me to have emotions of joy, while other sad stories may signal a temporary emotion of sadness.

What I have just described is normal in the life of any human. In the life of an individual who has successfully battled and coped with bipolar illness, they have learned how to minimize the effect of the emotion. Whether the emotion is joyful or filled with sadness, the individual with bipolar success does not automatically remain in those emotions for a prolonged time.

Bipolar disorder is a psychological disease that is always manifested in the sufferer's behavior and emotions, which ultimately form in their minds and brains. Hence, it is typically referred to as a chemical imbalance. In the brain and mind, emotional triggers may develop.

Once those triggers turn into emotions, a psychological storm can ensue. The storm brewing within the depressed individual's mental state becomes the genesis of the manic or depressive episode. While the mental storm is occurring, the affected individual is not their usual self, which can result in behavior that is not typical of that individual.

After the mental storm, the depressed individual, the doctor/therapist, and the individual's support system must gradually rebuild the mind and brain to where they commenced originally. The rebuilding of the mind must occur for the bearer of the severe mental disorder to experience some semblance of mental wellness. Once the mind and brain recover from the mental storm's aftermath, coping with bipolar disorder successfully is not far from occurring.

Understanding bipolar illness itself is crucial for the affected individual to experience mental health success. If they are oblivious to their condition, then they cannot successfully cope with it. They should desire to learn everything there is to know about their mental disorder.

Some of those who are diagnosed with bipolar disorder do not care to learn about the psychological condition. When this occurs, their chances of overcoming this mental illness decrease. No individual who has battled bipolar disorder for a long time should not at least have some semblance of knowledge about their psychiatric disease.

The more knowledge that the mentally affected individual gains about their mental condition, the better equipped they can become to be more mentally redeemed. Today, there is no excuse that the bearer of bipolar disorder can give when it comes to acquiring knowledge about their psychological condition. Their psychiatrists/therapists have a wealth of knowledge.

These mental health professionals and experts are there to help guide individuals who are having challenges and difficulties with their mental wellness to become more mentally aware of how to cope with them successfully. In other words, the depressed person's doctor or therapist must be viewed as the individual who can teach the mentally affected individual all the signs and symptoms of what this mental illness entails. Attending regular doctor's visits, whether it is face-to-face or by a computer screen, is imperative for the bearer of bipolar disorder to gain more insight into their illness.

Regaining mental health is the goal for all who are afflicted with any type of mental disorder. Without the acquisition of knowledge, the afflicted individual can potentially remain in that same mental state. A bearer of bipolar disorder must not become reluctant to ask the mental health provider tough questions. Posing difficult questions can help the bearer become more confident in asking more of them. An individual's path to mental wellness and success is clearer when they are not timid. Bipolar disorder is successfully fought when knowledge and understanding are the sufferer's ammunition.

The depressed individual must not allow embarrassment and discomfort to dictate whether or not questions should be posed. One must have the mindset and attitude that there is no such thing as an "unintelligent question." All questions about one's mental recovery from bipolar disorder are pertinent and valid, so no bearer should feel any kind of guilt or shame. An individual's mental health and recovery are at stake, and acquiring knowledge about the signs, symptoms, and treatment of one's psychological illness is always beneficial.

Monitoring the depressed individual's progress is helpful in coping with this psychological condition. It should not always be reserved for the psychiatrist/therapist, but the bearer must also keep a personal inventory of how they are doing mentally. As I previously mentioned in an earlier chapter, daily journaling will drastically and significantly help the bearer express feelings and emotions.

There is a psychological benefit to having one's feelings written down on paper. An individual coping with bipolar disorder or any other mental illness can always revert to how they felt during a particular time in their life. My hope for any individual who is living with and coping with this psychological disorder is that their progress or improvement is always headed in a positive direction. When depressed individuals are journaling each day, they can instantly determine whether or not their mental health progression is going well or not.

Successfully coping with bipolar disorder always requires periodic monitoring from one's psychiatrist/therapist. The dread of attending therapy and counseling sessions will not prove beneficial when striving to acquire mental health success. In fact, the mindset and attitude toward therapy for mental illnesses, such as bipolar disorder, are just as crucial to one's mental recovery and success as taking the prescribed psychotropic medicine.

Living with a psychological illness does not have to be an ongoing feeling of guilt or shame. Individuals who are successfully monitored every so often by their mental health provider can potentially be mentally strong despite what others may gather. Depressed individuals who realize the importance of lifelong monitoring will not have an issue with it.

Instead, they will welcome being monitored by their doctor with great anticipation. As a depressed individual, I love checking in with my psychiatrist every few months to let him know that I am mentally thriving and coping successfully with my psychological condition. Personally, I would rather be monitored by a mental health physician than not be monitored at all.

Improving mentally is not the only goal for anyone who has had a psychotic break in the past. The individual who is coping with bipolar disorder should not become lax and content with only temporary mental recovery. Real recovery is when the depressed person's mental health is successfully coped with continuously while being monitored from time to time.

All individuals who have been diagnosed with bipolar disorder should not hesitate to be monitored by a board-certified and licensed psychiatrist. It is through periodic monitoring that the depressed individual's mental health improvement and success can be documented and charted. For the affected individual who has experienced months or even years of mental success, there is deep mental satisfaction when the psychological disease is monitored and under control.

Having a mental illness in today's world is now viewed as manageable. Bipolar illness can also be put in that same category. Coping successfully with this psychological disorder is definitely not a dream or a fantasy.

Society, as a whole, is collectively considering the fact that bipolar disorder, as well as other mental illnesses, is not the "end of the road" for the bearer. It has recently become established in the modern world and society we presently reside in that any individual who desires to overcome the symptoms and triggers of bipolar disorder can. They must first become motivated and determined to do what is required of them to achieve mental stability. If the process of remaining mentally stable is welcomed, then I am certain that mental success and recovery will ensue. There is nothing special or out of the ordinary that a depressed individual must do to become successful in coping with their mental health.

Sometimes, an individual can make the coping process more difficult than it has to be. For example, having anxiety and worry over issues and problems that one cannot control will negatively affect the depressed individual's quest to cope with bipolar disorder. In our lives, mishaps and challenges will inevitably occur without any warning.

Those who are bearers of bipolar illness must somehow strive to live their lives successfully while also coping with a psychological disorder, from which one can potentially fall ill again. One who has successfully overcome bipolar disease for a long time does not allow oneself to think continuously about manic and depressive episodes of yesteryear. When bipolar individuals spend their time living each day without focusing on their psychological illness, the illness' lingering effects will become minimal.

In my opinion, a depressed individual can be empowered psychologically when there are continuous days of mental wellness and consistency. After the individual is mentally inspired to continue to psychologically thrive, there will be no limit to the amount of mental health success that they can potentially experience. For many years, I have been fortunate and blessed enough to know that I am not alone in my mental wellness path and journey.

Some people in this current world are advocates for all of the individuals who are in the mentally ill community. Individuals who are champions for the psychologically afflicted would love to see those who have been mentally affected by their respective psychological afflictions succeed in coping with them. Though every individual who has ever been diagnosed with a mental disorder can potentially face struggle and an uphill battle, that does not mean that they are a failure.

I personally believe it is a success if the individual attempts to combat the psychological disease with all of their might and strength. In life, many have become successful despite a plethora of failed attempts. The real barometer of true success with regard to coping with bipolar disorder is not the attempt to cope but the ability of the bearer to continue to combat the illness nonstop.

Faith, commitment, and perseverance will never equate to anyone becoming unsuccessful in life. This same concept can be applied to an individual who has successfully battled bipolar disorder. Before a mentally affected individual can enjoy continuous mental health success, they must first develop a plan to succeed.

Planning for consistency in mental wellness commences and ends with the afflicted individual's thoughts. Although support groups, mental health advocates, friends, and loved ones can influence a depressed person's mental health success, they are not always the determining factors of the desired outcome. Bearers of bipolar disorder must somehow acquire the motivation to be dedicated to coping successfully with the mental disorder.

The one thing that all mentally affected individuals should do to enjoy mental bliss and victory is to think about and envision their dream scenario with regard to mental wellness and success. Some may envision a day when they do not have to take psychotropic medications. But the dream or vision for mental health success as a whole is, in the grand scheme of things, greater than that.

Medicine alone does not always control all of the triggers and symptoms of either a manic or depressive episode, but it is only a portion of a successful journey. But the consumption of psychotropic medicine cannot guarantee mental wellness and stability because, if it is not taken properly, it will not be as effective. Now I am not at all stating that taking the prescribed medicine is ineffective.

What I am trying to convey is that the sufferer has to also have a mindset of commitment and determination to mentally recover. A purpose-driven attitude and mindset, along with taking the prescribed medicine and therapy, will ultimately pay off in the end. The end result of an individual who is motivated and perseveres usually equates to the individual reaching their dreams and goals.

When it comes to the dream scenario of an individual who has battled bipolar disorder in the past, or currently, I am certain that they would prefer to experience mental relief and comfort continuously. In previous years, when I was in the midst of a bipolar struggle, I was not a proponent of taking the prescribed medicine. Now I am definitely a fan of taking it. My cooperation in taking the psychotropic drugs, along with my optimistic attitude and mindset, has been vital to my mental health turnaround and success.

If an individual who is living with and coping with bipolar disorder is to become successful in their mental disorder, then they must learn how to seize the opportunity to become mentally well and whole. Having a psychiatrist or therapist willing to help them experience prolonged mental health is the bearer's best chance to regain their mind. All that is required with that opportunity is the affected individual's overall effort.

Exercising at least three times a week will significantly affect a bearer's mood positively. There is nothing better than releasing one's energy and anxiety through a regular exercise routine. I believe that daily exercise has definitely been one of the contributing factors to my ability to successfully live with and cope with bipolar disorder for several years.

Initially, if a depressed individual is not used to being physically active, exercising regularly can be a bit of a chore rather than a fun activity. In my experience with exercise, I always feel better after I work out. Basically, I feel a sense of accomplishment when my workout is completed, and also, exercising consistently gives me the courage to face the world. An individual who has battled and won over bipolar illness cannot be victorious and successful over it by just sitting around and not moving their body.

An active mind and body typically result in good health. Not too many physically active individuals are unhealthy unless they are stricken with a rare illness or disorder. I personally urge all individuals who are mentally affected by bipolar disorder to engage in some kind of physical activity.

When the depressed person has an active life, they will potentially enjoy mental success. What I mean by an active life is a life of seeking dreams and goals. No one can achieve any kind of aspiration in life by being inactive.

Individuals who have been coping successfully with bipolar disorder for a long time have overcome the mental struggle that is part of the illness. Mental success is achieved when the mind is free from the disease's psychological hold and grasp. Exercising regularly and having a consistent nightly sleep routine can help the mind and brain function at their optimum level.

Once exercise, sleep, and setting realistic dreams and goals are established, the psychologically affected individual will be able to cope successfully with bipolar disorder, hopefully with a minimum of setbacks. The key to experiencing continuous mental health success is doing those activities that I just stated with persistence and perseverance.

Some of those who are unsuccessful in coping with bipolar disorder give up on performing the daily activities that can ultimately help them to remain mentally well and consistent. Consistency, perseverance, and motivation are the driving forces behind accomplishing anything in life that one may desire. Those who desire to have success in coping with bipolar disorder must continue to develop their plan for mental wellness.

This requires mental courage and strength, which we all have within ourselves. A depressed individual may surprise himself or herself when mental health success finally comes to fruition. But first, the path or journey into one's mental wellness and recovery has to become consistent and steady.

Very few people understand how living with bipolar disorder is not as difficult as it can be initially. To all of the individuals in the bipolar community, I suggest that you do not give up on one day having consistency in mental wellness. Whether you realize this known fact or not, bipolar disorder can be controlled, treated, and coped with successfully.

Once the challenge of discovering the right kind of psychotropic medications to take subsides, the road or path for mental consistency and success is not as wide anymore. The depressed individual must do their part if they want to remain on that mental health wellness journey. In counseling and therapy sessions, the affected individual should work on their whole self.

As a depressed person myself, it took years of self-assessment and examination before I discovered a mental health breakthrough. My mental breakthrough occurred when I commenced to focus on the true person that I am inside. All bipolar individuals must distinguish themselves from the psychological illness itself and the individual at their core.

My hope for all who have struggled and battled bipolar disorder is to not lose themselves. The world and society will label and tell someone who they are without ever knowing the real person. So if you happen to have bipolar illness, you have a decision to make.

One has the choice of allowing others to define you by your mental disorder or by the genuine person you truly are. Now I am cognizant of the fact that many in the bipolar community loathe the side effects of taking the prescribed psychotropic medicine. I must also state that I am not the biggest proponent of the negative side effects that occur from continuous consumption.

All medicine has side effects, no matter what health condition it is generally prescribed for. Taking medicine for a chemical imbalance does not define the core of any individual. What medicine taken for an illness, such as bipolar disorder, does is help bring out the true personality of that individual. There is nothing wrong with getting a mental boost from something that will ultimately help an individual experience years or even decades of mental stability.

An individual's mental livelihood and wellness should never be predicated on the side effects of taking psychotropic medicine if the side effects are minimal and will help the bearer of the psychological condition enjoy prolonged mental and emotional wellness and success. There are no limitations to overall success for the individual who is dedicated to their mental health. Success in this world is based on materialism, but true success is when the individual is enjoying joy and contentment in life without worrying about how others will perceive them.

Brighter days are in store for the individual who learns how to successfully cope with this psychological illness. Though externally, the world in which we live is increasingly covered in darkness and despair, those who are dealing with bipolar disorder do not have to live with hopelessness. They can experience the same joy in life as nonbearers.

I am fully aware that sustaining mental wellness and health can become difficult in the midst of all of the world's tragic occurrences. A depressed individual must strive not to become influenced and mentally affected by all of the chaos continuously plaguing society. The issues and problems of society should not have any effect on any individual's ability to experience mental health success.

As long as societal issues do not have a direct effect on one's mental wellness and recovery, a bearer can successfully experience life's best. Yes, they deserve to enjoy all of the worthwhile and beautiful things that life can bring. The only requirement that they should have is experiencing the joys of life with an open mind. A life filled with mental bliss is a result of the individual successfully coping with the psychological condition. Coping with bipolar disorder is a continuous, lifelong process.

Once a depressed individual is diagnosed with a psychological illness, they must immediately prepare to cope. Successfully coping with bipolar disorder should always be their top priority and goal. They do not have to experience any kind of mental health failure when it comes to coping with the condition for a long time.

At the time that I am writing this book, it seems as though the current pandemic is gradually having less of an impact than it did previously. Hopefully, the anxiety and despair that have surrounded the world and society for over a year will not drastically affect the mental health of the masses. Regardless of whether or not a global pandemic remains prevalent in the world and society or becomes less of a significant issue, mental illnesses, such as bipolar disorder, will continue to affect millions in this country as well as worldwide.

Because the mental disorder has been gradually increasing over the years, it is now more imperative than ever that bearers of this psychological illness become mentally armed with all of the tools and coping skills to successfully combat it. Let's face it. If you are diagnosed with bipolar illness, you will have to somehow discover how to overcome it. The only way to successfully treat it besides talk therapy is through the consumption of psychotropic medicine, which has proven to be effective.

Of course, I will be the first to tell you that I am highly unqualified to comment on the efficacy of psychiatric drugs, but as an individual who has taken other medicines for the mental disease, some worked well while others did not. Each depressed individual has various reactions to the prescribed medicines. When a particular medicine is effective, never hesitate to take it consistently as prescribed because its positive effect will serve as a catalyst for a healthy and successful cognitive thought pattern.

Rising from the depths of mental agony and anguish is the final outcome of the individual's mental health success and consistency. Mental wellness is what all who suffer from bipolar disorder should focus on in life. When they become mentally well, in most instances, they can experience all facets of life.

There is no such thing as a life void of experiencing some form of health ailment or condition. An individual is fortunate if he or she only has one health issue or concern to contend with. Bipolar disorder should be viewed in the same way that other medical conditions are viewed, though the condition is mental.

In recent years, the stigma of an individual being bipolar has improved. The psychological disorder and its bearers have become humanized. At the end of the day, all who suffer from bipolar illness also have feelings. Not all who happen to suffer from a mental illness are "barbaric" in nature. Bipolar individuals can also be the sweetest, gentlest, and kindest of souls.

Today, the face of bipolar disorder can be your next-door neighbor or that quiet person you might see in passing. Because of the evolution of medicine for mental illnesses, in some instances, bearers might not exhibit behaviors that pose a threat to themselves and others. I credit the medicines and advancements in research with regard to mental illnesses, such as bipolar disorder, for helping many bipolar individuals cope with the psychiatric condition with great assurance.

The life of an individual who is afflicted with bipolar illness does not have to become a sad one. Support in this present age can only be a few clicks away on the affected individual's personal computer. Virtual support—although interpersonal support is more favorable—can also help the depressed individual.

It is better to at least have virtual support coming from a computer screen rather than receiving no kind of support at all. Individuals who are mindful that they have support tend to excel psychologically and emotionally. It is when the mentally affected individual realizes that they have loving support that coping successfully with bipolar disorder is possible.

My hope for any individual who is currently battling with bipolar disorder and experiencing difficulties and adversity because of it is to never abandon their hope. With hope, there is always an expectation that is fulfilled. It is also the attainment of potential.

If you, as a bearer of bipolar disorder, do not disregard your hope that mental success and wellness can be obtained and acquired, then coping successfully with this psychological illness will occur and fall into place. I wholeheartedly believe that with the right motivation, it will be achieved. This will require full commitment and devotion to one's mental health, which must have full precedence in the life of the bearer.

Romain U. DuFour III is the author of five literary works ranging from Christianity to child bullying to self-help psychology. DuFour III writes about a subject matter that is prevalent in today's society. He strongly believes that many of the literary topics he has written about can eventually be overcome with a positive and willing mindset. The goal that DuFour III would like to convey in his writings is the sustainability of maintaining inner peace and joy in a world of negativity.